CONTENTS

	Introduction	
	Cassette details	6
	Notes on speaking and listening	6
	Notes on reading	7
	Notes on writing	8
UNIT 1	Details and analysis in terms of the NC	10
	Aims	
	Notes on activities	
	Page for photocopying (essential)	
UNIT 2	Details and analysis in terms of the NC	14
	Aims	
	Notes on activities	
	Page for photocopying (optional)	
UNIT 3	Details and analysis in terms of the NC	18
	Aims	
	Notes on activities	
	Pages for photocopying (one essential)	
UNIT 4	Details and analysis in terms of the NC	26
	Aims	
	Notes on activities	
	Pages for photocopying (optional)	
UNIT 5	Details and analysis in terms of the NC	30
	Aims	
	Notes on activities	
	Pantomime script (optional)	
UNIT 6	Details and analysis in terms of the NC	38
	Aims	
	Notes on activities	
	Pages for photocopying (optional)	
UNIT 7	Details and analysis in terms of the NC	43
	Aims	
	Notes on activities	
UNIT 8	Details and analysis in terms of the NC	45
	Aims	
	Notes on activities	
UNIT 9	Details and analysis in terms of the NC	47
	Aims	
	Notes on activities	
	Pages for photocopying (optional)	
UNIT 10	Details and analysis in terms of the NC	51
	Aims	
	Notes on activities	
	Transcript of short story	

PUNCTUATION	Notes		59
	Photocopiable worksheets	– Sentences	60
	"	– Question marks	61
	"	– Capital letters	62
	"	– Speech marks	63
	"	– Paragraphs	65
SPELLING	Introduction and Overview		66
	Photocopiable worksheets	– short vowel	69
	"	– initial blends	71
	"	– final blends	73
	"	– triple blends	76
	"	– plurals	77
	"	– final "e"	78
	"	– past tense	80
	"	– vowel digraph "ee"	81
	Record keeping charts		83

INTRODUCTION

Each book in the series is divided into three sections: thematic units; punctuation and spelling.

Units
Information about each unit in the Pupil's Book is given in the Teacher's Pack. The information consists of:
- analysis of Pupil's Book and Teacher's Pack activities in terms of SOA's
- details of useful further resources in the Teacher's Pack or on cassette
- list of aims of each activity
- extension activities
- notes on activities
- photocopiable pages

Activities: The numbering and lettering system
Each unit in the Pupil's Book contains about 7–10 numbered activities. Many of these activities have been extended in the Teacher's Pack to provide a range of further material. Where this happens the extension activities are given the number of the Pupil's Book activity that they relate to, but are further marked by a letter. For example, in Unit 2 of the Pupil's Book, Activity 5 has two extension activities in the Teacher's Pack and these two activities are referred to as 5A and 5B respectively.

Analysis of Statements of Attainment
Each activity in the Pupil's Book and Teacher's Pack is analysed in terms of the Statements of Attainment (SOA's). The SOA's have been detailed in the light of current information; changes, developments and clarifications may render some of the information on the SOA's out of date in the future. The right hand column in the Analysis chart indicates SOA's, above or below levels 2 and 3 or in attainment target 4 which are covered by activities in the Unit. Extension activities in the Teacher's Pack are shown in the tinted panels.

Further resources
Also at the beginning of each unit, there is a grid giving details so that the teacher can see at a glance whether a PHOTOCOPY needs to be made or the CASSETTE TAPE is needed or whether there are NOTES available for further information on any given activity. CASSETTE details mainly state when a cassette recording is available, whether it is essential or whether the information on the cassette could be presented another way to avoid using a tape recorder, e.g. the teacher could read the poem or two pupils read a transcript of an interview, etc.

Punctuation and spelling
The activities in the Punctuation and Spelling sections of the Pupil's Book are designed on the assumption that the pupils will be putting their work into exercise books or on loose pages for inclusion in a folder. In the Teacher's Pack however, the activities have been organised so that the sheets can be photocopied, written on by the pupil and used for homework if required. On the whole, the activities in the Pupil's Book in punctuation and spelling are repeated in the Teacher's Pack, in some cases extending the information, at other times providing the same information but in a different way.

The cassette
Where possible, material on the cassette has been transcribed so that if a tape recorder breaks down or is not available, the teacher or pupils can read the transcript instead. Cassette details are given on the page following this introduction.

CASSETTE DETAILS

UNIT 1
Activity 6
A Sound effects: house and street sounds, which are described in the poem in activity 7. (Details of what these are can be found in the notes for Unit 1.)

Activity 7
B Poem: Half Asleep

UNIT 2
Activity 1
C Poem: Irritating Sayings

UNIT 3
Activity 4
D Poem: The Computer's First Christmas Card

UNIT 5
Activity 1
E(i) Start of ACT TWO of the Play — (stop for anticipation)
E(ii) Three more minutes of the play to hear what happened next

Activity 4
E(iii) Completion of ACT TWO

UNIT 8
Activity 3
F Sound effects: fairground

UNIT 10
Activity 1
G Short story

NOTES ON SPEAKING AND LISTENING

The precise nature of the groupings for speaking and listening activities and the method of approach has not always been specified or has been kept at the "partner" stage, particularly in Book 1. The reason for this is that the type of arrangement made will very much depend on the children and their previous experience of oral and shared work.

Many pupils coming up from junior school will already have had experience of a range of class groupings and of the ground "rules" for discussion.

For those pupils for whom this is not the case, however, it is best to start slowly and establish some of the ground rules for discussion and collaborative work before embarking on group work.

The range of options for grouping children include:
- with a friend
- mixed ability
- single sexed group
- similar ability
- mixed sexes

Other factors are also involved, for example the role of the teacher, whether the pupils are bilingual or multilingual and the kind of activities they are engaged in.

Initially for pupils unused to working in groups, working with a friend provides a good introduction. Before starting this it might be helpful to ask the children what they think the benefit of working with a friend might be and for the teacher's view to be given, as well.

Before starting activities with a larger group, basic ground rules need to be established. This can be done by asking the pupils what they think the ground rules should be in a given task, e.g. where the pupils are grouped together to spark off ideas in order to expand a topic or where they collaborate together to negotiate a consensus. They usually derive some of the main points, e.g. listening to one another, not talking at the same time, making sure everyone who wants to speak, does so. Teachers can than add additional guidelines, or some group work could proceed and then further ground rules be derived by the pupils in the light of experience.

As pupils become more skilled, the guidelines can be extended to include for example, picking up a point raised by a pupil and expanding it, listening to an argument and putting forward another view point.

After working in various groups over two or three weeks, it can be useful for pupils to discuss what they feel the value of this kind of learning to be and for the teacher to express what he/she thinks can be gained. Pupils do not always realise the value of oral work.

As pupils gain experience, they can take on specific roles e.g.

Chairperson
Note taker
Pupil responsible for summarising the group views when groups come together for class discussion
Pupil visiting another group to listen to their ideas with the aim of returning to base and inputting information gained
The pupil elected to listen to a group discussion/collaboration in order to analyse what has been happening and to provide feedback to the group.

To help develop skills further, pupils can keep a talking/listening record or a talking diary. For comprehensive details of this and much more: Talking and Learning 5 to 16, an in-service pack on oracy by the Open University and the National Oracy project.

NOTES ON READING

Overview
The tips and suggestions on these pages aim to help pupils who have been through primary education and who still have some problems with reading.

Missing suffixes
If suffixes are incorrectly read or omitted e.g. dog/dogs; sit/sitting, and this type of miscue occurs fairly regularly, one method that can help is to make a work sheet from a text which the pupil reads at independent/instructional level and delete some or all of the suffixes. Sometimes sixth formers or pupils in the typing department are prepared to type out such a text. Gradually a bank of texts at different levels will amass for future use. Alternatively, a passage could be photocopied and tippexed, though this is not ideal.

Reading over full stops
This can prevent the pupil from extracting the full meaning of what is being read. One way to help is for the pupil to ring round in pencil all of the full stops in the next four paragraphs or in one or two pages, before reading to the teacher, partner or into a tape. Another method is to ask the pupil to take two breaths at each full stop, or nod his/her head or similar. Obviously this would only be done for thirty seconds or so when the pupil is reading to the teacher, but it causes much amusement and does make the point.

Omissions and additions
Although seemingly not too important a problem, particularly when the pupil adjusts what has been read to retain continuity of tense, etc., additions and omissions can nevertheless alter meaning. Self monitoring, using a tape recorder or working with a partner can be useful or the cloze procedure where every seventh letter is deleted can also help.

Miscues where the substitutions are non-words or meaning is lost
If pupils are giving options that are unrelated to the meaning, then the pupil is not reading for meaning. If the reading is at independent level, perhaps the book is still too hard for fluency and prediction to be possible, or perhaps the pupil has forgotten the purpose of reading and is concentrating too much on getting the words "right". Appropriate action depends on the reasons for the problem, but of all the outcomes this is the most serious.

Perhaps it is time to remind the pupil of the pleasures that books can bring by arranging for the pupil to listen to tapes of books. This could be followed by choosing a book that has been enjoyed and that is not too hard to read, and arranging for paired reading of the book.

Substitutions where the letter order is incorrect
Where the word substituted has the same letters but in a different order, eg. being/begin; tired/tried, it might be that the pupil does not appreciate the relevance of letter order. If this is a regular miscue the pupil might benefit from activities that highlight the effect of letter order, such as work with anagrams, or choosing between words such as pets/pest in a structured cloze test.

Problems with visually similar words
If pupils have problems with visually similar words such as ever/even; look/took; sigh/sign, check the print of the book that the pupil is reading. Although it happens less now, publishers still sometimes pick print which minimises the differences between letters, e.g. ascenders and descenders are short or there are no serifs. If print is not the problem then it can be helpful to discuss the similarities between the words with the pupil and re-emphasise the role of prediction.

Letter/word reversals
To what extent letter/word order reversals are a problem, e.g. b/d; was/saw; month/mouth, can depend on how much successful reading experience the pupil has had. New readers often have these problems and as reading experience is gained these problems diminish and stop.

If this does not happen and there are other problems such as confusing visually similar words, letter order problems and spelling problems, it may be worth checking to see if the pupil has a specific learning difficulty.

Substitutions or refusals which reveal poor phonic knowledge
Some children may benefit from using a phonic strategy in reading. Where this is the case and knowledge of phonics is poor, a short time set aside to focus on a phonic rule can be very helpful. This could be done when listening to a pupil read. One phonic rule can be taken at a time using some of the suggestions in the spelling section — numbers 3 and 4 — but applying these to reading.

NOTES ON WRITING

For many pupils with learning problems, writing can seem a daunting task. It can help if pupils realise that not everything they write has to be perfectly presented or even seen by the teacher, and not everything subjected to drafting and re-drafting. When pupils think that everything they write is going to go through a number of drafting processes or be marked for spelling and handwriting, then those pupils who are able to write quite a large amount invariably cut the quantity down because either they cannot face working on drafts of such length or face the array of red ink highlighting spelling and punctuation errors. Other pupils may avoid the use of good vocabulary, picking a synonym which they know they can spell but which is far less apt or may avoid using the word altogether. The purposes of writing are important for all writers, but for pupils with learning problems they take on a particular significance.

Tape recorders
In some cases, such as writing short stories, poems and articles, the process of writing includes the ideas behind the writing outcome; the translation of these ideas into the format required and the process of getting all of this on to paper. Some pupils with learning problems have very good ideas and are quick to learn some of the skills required for specific writing outcomes but have severe difficulties getting all of this on to paper. Pupils with this kind of problem often start their writing task very well but lose the thread of what they

wanted to say and lose heart in the middle or put very little down in the first place; yet, if their ideas could be written down for them, they could produce a very good piece of work.

These pupils in particular could benefit from sometimes using a tape recorder, initially to record ideas and then to record the final format, e.g. a short story or poem. When the pupil is satisfied with the outcome, he/she can then translate it on to paper. By having everything recorded, the writing task is reduced to a dictation exercise and the pupil can concentrate on handwriting, spelling and presentation in general. Just occasionally a scribe could be used so that the pupil will not be discouraged from writing everything they want to say because of the writing load that would result.

It is important for this kind of pupil to realise that just because they have problems with getting ideas on to paper does not mean that they cannot write a good short story or poem, or that their contribution is in any way less worthy because they have used different means for arriving at an outcome.

Note-taking

It is important for pupils to realise that a lot of their writing is to record ideas or make notes and that these can be jotted down in a rough book and are for their eyes only. Freed of worries about spelling, handwriting and presentation, pupils can then concentrate on the ideas to be recorded.

Brainstorming and planning

To help at the ideas stage of writing, pupils with learning problems can benefit from brainstorming techniques, jotting down thoughts, words, arguments, etc, and then imposing order on these at a later stage using coloured pens to link ideas/words that share a theme. Similarly, making a plan such as deciding what each paragraph is going to cover in an article helps to order thoughts with minimal writing.

Drafting

Drafting and re-drafting have a very important role in certain kinds of writing. It is important for pupils to realise how writing can develop at various stages of the drafting process and that this is a process that professional writers go through.

Once the purpose of drafting has been recognised it can be valuable for pupils to share the activity with each other, as well as with an adult.

The word processor and other sources

The word processor can be very helpful in a number of cases. For example, pupils for whom tape-recorders are helpful can often be greatly helped writing directly onto the word processor particularly if there is a spell check facility as well.

The word processor can be very rewarding for those children who find it hard to produce material of any length and maintain a high standard of presentation and for all pupils it is very satisfying to see work look professional. As well as pupils using the word processor themselves other people can sometimes help. Very often the typing department of the school has students who are prepared to type out work presented to them. Sixth formers often elect to spend time helping teachers of pupils with learning problems and may be happy to type out work. Some small businesses in the locality with word processors/printing facilities are sometimes pleased to produce small booklets of short stories, etc. free of charge or for a small sum. It is worth making enquiries.

UNIT 1 PEOPLE AND PLACES

Further Resources Available

Activity number	Cassette material	Alternative to cassette	Photocopiable material	Alternative to photocopy	Notes
1					p 12
6	Sound effects				p 12
7	Poem	Pupil or teacher could read this			p 12
10			p 13		p 12

Analysis of Activities

Statements of Attainment	LEVEL 2 a	b	c	d	e	f	LEVEL 3 a	b	c	d	e	f	SOA'S COVERED Act	SOA	
SPEAKING + LISTENING **1**			6,7										7	1b	PB
															TP
READING **2**					1,2 3,7 8,9					7			9	4b	PB
															TP
WRITING **3**				4											PB
										5A					TP

Key to charts
PB = Pupil's Book   TP = Teacher's Pack
▓ = Extension activities in TP   SOA = Statement of Attainment

Aims of Unit 1

ACTIVITIES	AIMS
1	To gain experience of a format found in many popular magazines and comics for young people.
2	To encourage understanding of a short text and in the process gain further experience of the conventions of a chart.
3	To widen understanding of personality charts by encouraging pupils to think about and discuss other questions that could (and could not) go on to a chart.
4	To provide the opportunity for writing about themselves in an interesting and enjoyable way and to present their work attractively for a class display for themselves and their class.
5	To build on the experience gained in the first two activities by reading an animal chart and making their own animal charts to add to the display.
5A	To collaborate together and take responsibility for mounting a display so gaining experience of how to make an attractive and eye-catching presentation.
6	To help develop listening skills by identifying and interpreting a range of everyday household and street sounds and to provide a framework for listening to the poem "Half Asleep".
7	To listen to and enjoy a poem and to encourage awareness of the way a poet sets a scene, here by describing household and street sounds.
8	To encourage careful reading of a poem.
9	To gain further understanding of a poem by looking at it in more detail and to encourage an informed personal response.
10	Role A: to encourage careful observation and accurate description. Role B: to encourage careful listening and accurate observation. For some pupils this will just provide the opportunity for structured talking and listening, with specific aims depending on the children involved, e.g. the child who tends to use mostly nouns and verbs when talking can concentrate on trying to express each picture using more complete phrases and sentences.

NOTES ON ACTIVITIES

ACTIVITY 1

The chart may need to be read to the pupils once or twice. Some pupils may have seen the format in magazines and comics, and this could be an opportunity for children to bring in similar examples, with the aim of creating interest in the written word.

EXTENSION ACTIVITY 5A

A group of pupils could be given the responsibility of organising a class display of the charts.

ACTIVITY 6

Sound effects on the cassette aim to convey the sounds the person in the poem can hear as they lie in bed with the windows open. The sounds are:

A toddler pretending to be a cross teacher by admonishing her teddy bears.
Two women chatting on the doorstep.
A tumble drier vibrating.
Someone playing a guitar.
A man trying to start his car.
A man tuning a motor bike.
Reggae music from an open window.
Children coming out of school.

ACTIVITY 7

Artist's "mistakes"
A There should be teddy bear s in the picture not dolls
B Mum should be chatting to the woman next door, not the milkman.
C A tumble drier should be vibrating, not a vacuum.
D A boy should be playing the guitar, not a girl.
E The man should be starting a car not a van.
F The bike sho uld be a Yamaha not a Suzuki.
G A reggae beat should be coming from the open window, not "Jingle Bells."
H The school is St John's not St Mark's.

ACTIVITY 10

The second pair of pictures give the opportunity to describe objects in a familiar situation; the first pictures ask the children to observe and interpret facial expression and body language. Further activities of this sort could be made by photocopying a clear lined drawing and changing and/or deleting some details and re-photocopying. The activity could extend vocabulary by using a range of pictures, e.g. canal/barge scene, haunted house with armour, etc. Observation and interpretation of expression and body language could be extended by using pictures with increasing degrees of nuance in them.

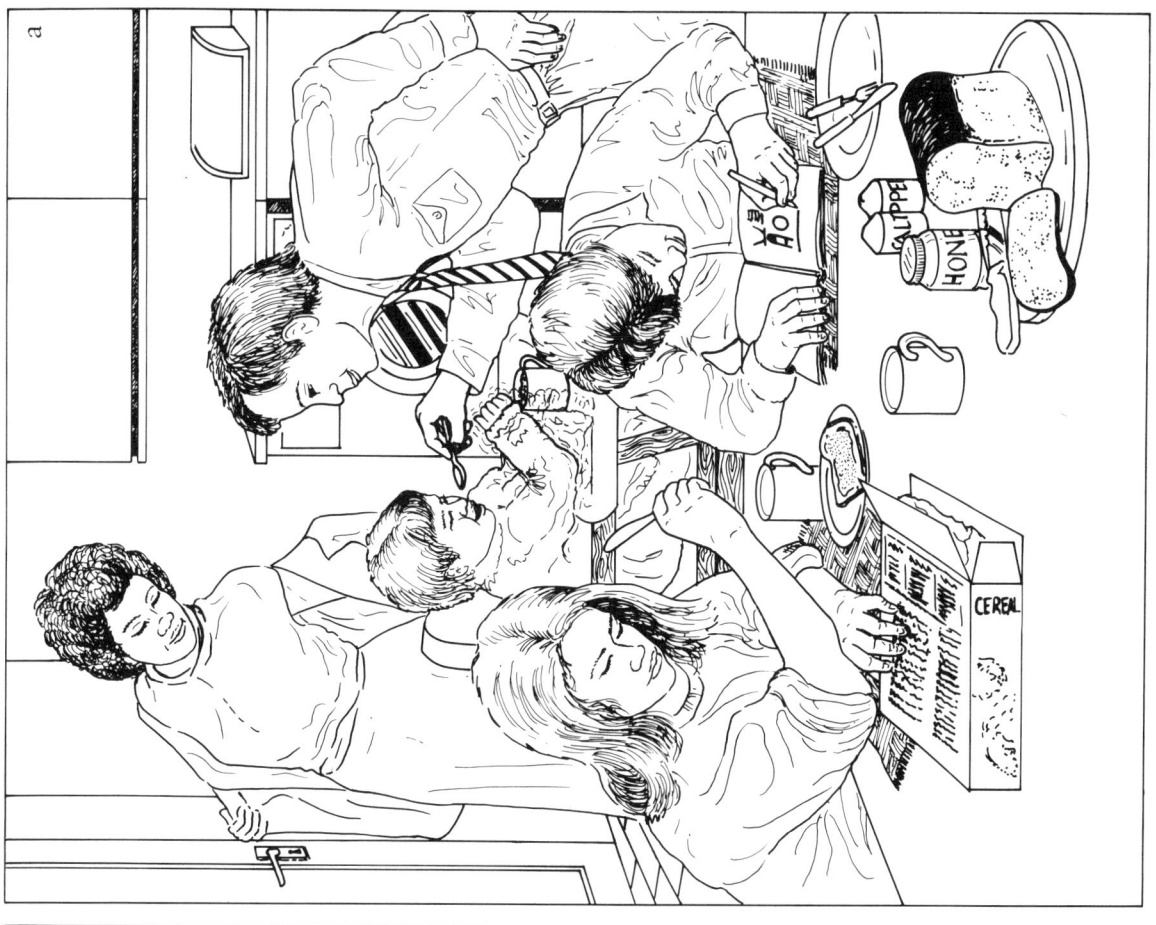

Resource Sheet 1   **Activity 10**

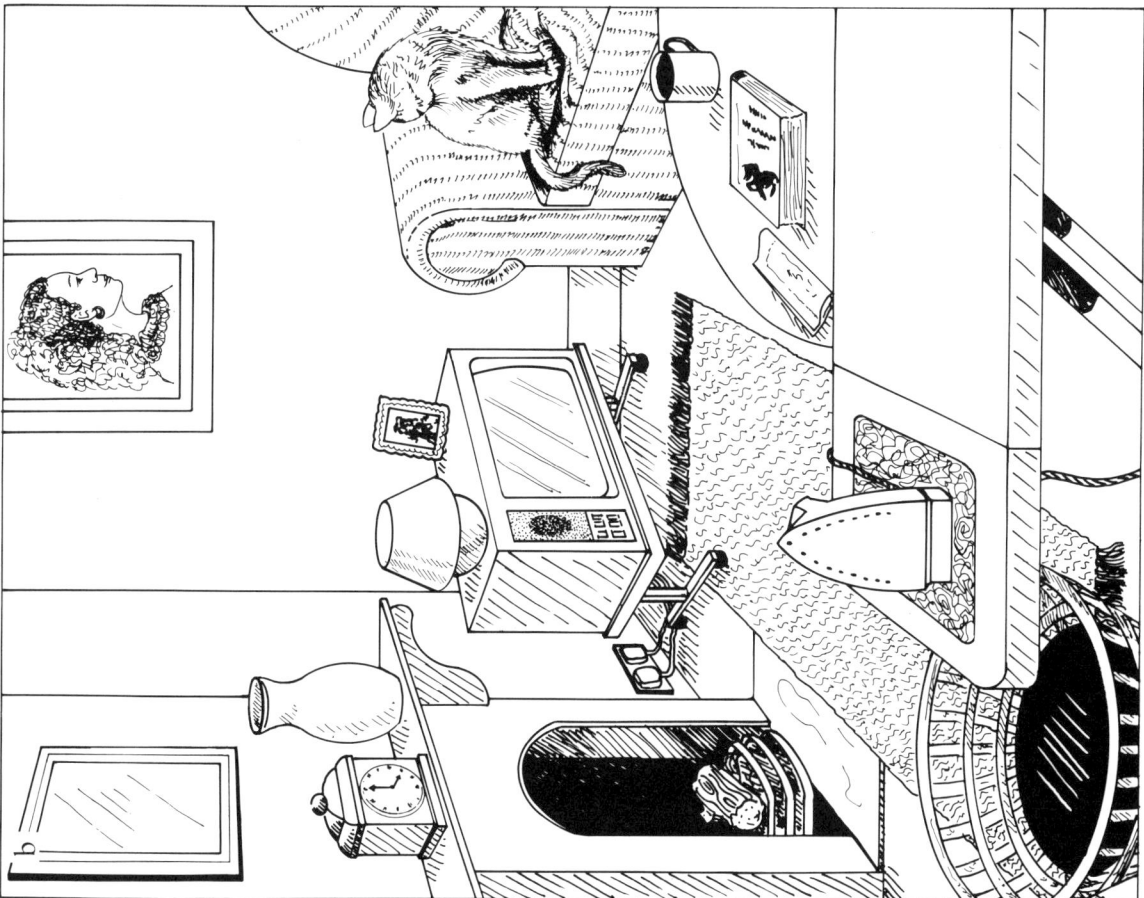

UNIT 1 People and Places —————— Highlight English —————— 13

UNIT 2 DO'S AND DON'TS

Further Resources Available

Activity number	Cassette material	Alternative to cassette	Photocopiable material	Alternative to photocopy	Notes
1	Poem	Pupil or teacher could read this			
5					p 16
6			p 17	Full text, in Pupil's Book as well	p 16
7					p 16

Analysis of Activities

Statements of Attainment	LEVEL 2						LEVEL 3						SOA'S COVERED		
	a	b	c	d	e	f	a	b	c	d	e	f	Act	SOA	
SPEAKING + LISTENING **1**		4, 5	1				4, 5						1	1b	PB
		3A 5A					3A 5A						3B	4c	TP
READING **2**					1					6, 7			6,7,8	4c	PB
															TP
WRITING **3**	9						9			2	9		2	4c	PB
					3B 5B					3B 5B			3B, 5B	4c	TP

Key to charts
PB = Pupil's Book   ▓ = Extension activities in TP
TP = Teacher's Pack   SOA = Statement of Attainment

Aims of Unit 2

ACTIVITIES	AIMS
1	To listen to and enjoy a poem. To encourage understanding of some of the sayings and so provide the opportunity for discussing and describing shared experiences in a very structured situation.
2	To write a poem together. By trial and error and discussion, to help develop an awareness of some of the criteria involved in putting a class poem together.
3	To read with a shared aim of presenting a class poem and providing the opportunity for reading with feeling, clarity and audibility.
3A and 3B	To draw on and extend the skills gained in the first three activites and provide the opportunity for pupils to use these skills to produce a similar poem on sayings. To help pupils see a familiar situation from a different perspective.
4	To encourage children to describe events and express opinions and personal feelings, and in the process develop skills as listeners and contributors in a discussion.
5	To encourage interest in presenting opinions and feelings succinctly and with clarity and in the process collaborate in a situation that requires some organisation, co-ordination and co-operation.
5A	To take the discussion further.
5B	To provide a light-hearted reason for writing for adults or other people in their household and to present work in an attractive and popular format.
6	To help develop awareness of some aspects of text, in a shared problem solving task.
7	To further understanding by looking at the paragraphs in the wider context of the story as a whole, using the title as a guide to aid prediction.
8	To encourage careful reading by focusing on the textual clues that link paragraphs.
9	To learn about, and gain experience of, some of the conventions of writing personal letters using a familiar topic which has been raised in activities 6, 7 and 8.

NOTES ON ACTIVITIES

EXTENSION ACTIVITY 3A

Activity 3 can be extended by children working in groups to discuss the things they say which they think might irritate their parents.

EXTENSION ACTIVITY 3B

Children could then work in groups or on their own, to put together these sayings to make a poem using the skills they have learned during ACTIVITY 3.

ACTIVITY 5

The kind of tape recorder with a built-in microphone is quite useful for this kind of activity. If the group is small, the children can sit in front of the microphone and when it is their turn to speak, just lean forward a little. Where the group is larger the pause button can be used, while a new set of children take seats in front of the microphone.

Where the microphone is separate, it is best to prop it up in a set position and then proceed as above.

Before beginning, children need to be sure they know what they are going to say, but not to write it down. When the tape recorder is on, each child takes it in turn to make his/her comment, leaving a small pause before the next person speaks.

The actual organisation and procedure then depends on the group. For example the teacher may prefer to make a recording then listen as a group to the results and agree some of the criteria for making a recording. Then, using the criteria, run through it again. Another procedure could be to discuss the criteria before making a recording. Where something goes wrong and a pupil wants to stop and start his/her contribution again, then that part of the tape could be erased for the pupil to try again.

Where appropriate, the children can organise themselves, decide on the order in which they will speak and decide what they will do if anything goes wrong, etc.

Examples of this type of recording can be found on Radio 5, in the evening, when young people often express their opinions in a similar format.

EXTENSION ACTIVITY 5A

Children could talk as a class or in small groups about the rules they would like to see the people in their house obey.

EXTENSION ACTIVITY 5B

Working on their own or in pairs, the children could write a set of "Rules of the House" written out and decorated to look like a charter.

ACTIVITY 6

PHOTOCOPYING

Paragraphs A – G for photocopying, page 17, can be cut out so that the children can manipulate the paragraphs physically and later can highlight key words and phrases. For a simpler task, paragraph G can be omitted.

Note: The readability of the paragraphs is fairly low, but as the two key words — "Form – rows" and "Lead" — are both homonyms it may be necessary to check that the children are making the correct option before engaging in the activity.

The order of paragraphs is: B, F, E, D, A, C, G

ACTIVITY 7

The book is about a headmaster who insists on complete and instant obedience to his rules. He uses his abnormal powers of hypnosis to control most of the students, but Dinah, the newcomer, helps to overthrow and expose his regime.

Resource Sheet 2 Activities 6 & 8

A

The tallest boy on the steps walked forward.
"Lead — in!" he shouted.
"Yes, Jeff," all the children said together.

B

Dinah walked on round the playground, waiting for the bell to ring or the whistle to go.

C

Still in silence, they began to march, row by row, up the steps and into the school. Their eyes were fixed in front of them and their feet kept in step. There was no giggling, or whispering or pushing. The only sound that you could hear was the tramping of feet.

D

"Yes, Rose," all the children said together. Then, like marching soldiers, they formed neat lines. Each child stood exactly a foot behind the one in front. Each line was exactly three feet from the one next to it. Not quite sure what to do, Dinah stood by herself.

E

There on the steps stood six children, three boys and three girls. They were all tall and they were all marked out from the others by a large white P on their blazer pockets. Without smiling, the tallest girl took a step forwards.

"Form — rows!" she yelled into the silence.

F

But there was no bell. No whistle. Nothing. All the sounds in the playground just stopped and the children turned round to stare at the school.

G

Dinah stood still, watching, until the playground was almost empty. As the last line marched off, she tacked herself on to the end of it and walked towards the school. When she got to the top of the steps, Rose stuck out her arm.

"Name?" she asked briskly.

"Dinah Glass," Dinah said. "I'm new and..."

UNIT 3 WORD GAMES

Further Resources Available

Activity number	Cassette material	Alternative to cassette	Photocopiable material	Alternative to photocopy	Notes
1			p 23	Teacher and pupils could make own.	p 20
1A					p 21
1B					p 21
1C					p 21
2			p 23		p 20
4	Poem	Pupil or teacher could read this.	p 24	Poem in PB. Photocopy for highlighting only.	p 21
5					p 21
7			p 25		p 22

Analysis of Activities

Statements of Attainment	LEVEL 2 a	b	c	d	e	f	LEVEL 3 a	b	c	d	e	f	SOA'S COVERED Act	SOA	
SPEAKING + LISTENING 1			4										1 4	4, 2d 1b	PB
	3A								3A	8A			1A	4, 2d	TP
READING 2				4			9			4			4 8 9	4b 5e 4a	PB
		1B 1C													TP
WRITING 3	3	3	3							6 8			3 6	4b 4c	PB
										8B					TP

Key to charts PB = Pupil's Book   ▨ = Extensions activities in TP   TP = Teacher's Pack   SOA = Statement of Attainment

Aims of Unit 3

ACTIVITIES	AIMS
1	To provide an interesting context for looking at the alphabet, extending and developing awareness of letters, letter order and dictionary skills. To encourage discussion on the criteria for selecting categories to go on the cards and so share the responsibility for developing a game.
1A, 1B, 1C	To increase understanding of the similarities and differences between letters in upper and lower case, knowledge of letter order, dictionary and ordering skills and provide a natural opportunity to use vocabulary associated with the alphabet.
2	To enjoy and co-operate in playing a game and in the process provide reasons for reading clearly and listening carefully and using knowledge of letter names. The whole to provide experience to be used for Activity 3.
3	To order experiences into a logical sequence to provide instructions on a subject that the children have been involved in.
3A	To encourage awareness of packaging and to collaborate in agreeing and producing a design.
4	To listen to and enjoy a poem. To further understanding of some aspects of poetry including rhyme, word meanings and the way words can be "played" with.
5	To play with letters and letter strings to form a list of words. To discuss the meanings and the sounds of the words and the criteria for selecting words for a poem.
6	To experience making choices and decisions about vocabulary in the process of writing a poem.
7	Role 1: to encourage careful observation and accurate description. Role 2: to encourage careful listening, help develop memory skills and give experience in recounting relevant information accurately. Role 3: to listen carefully and transpose verbal information into a visual format.
8	To learn about and extend understanding of a pun. To provide a purpose for writing and presenting material for themselves and the class.
8A	To collaborate together and take responsibility for a classroom display and so gain experience of making an attractive and eye-catching presentation.
8B	To encourage interest in magazines and comics for young people; encourage reading; encourage writing for a wider audience and to give purpose to addressing envelopes.
9	To encourage appreciation of the rhymes and rhythms of poetry and to appreciate the way voice can be used to convey meaning.
10	To provide the opportunity to read aloud to as high a standard as possible using the skills acquired in activity 9.

NOTES ON ACTIVITIES

ACTIVITIES 1 and 2

One of the aims of these activities is to provide material for writing instructions. By putting the details for making and playing the game in the Teacher's Book, the children work out the instructions from the experience.

ACTIVITY 1

In order to play the game, the children have to write out the letters of the alphabet and cut them out, or write out the letters of the alphabet on squares of paper. It is this part of the preparation for playing the game in particular, that can lead to a wealth of educational opportunities described on the next page.

To make the game (Resource Sheet 3A)
1. Each child writes out the letters of the alphabet on pieces of paper. Although only one set of letters of the alphabet is needed to play the game, the idea is that as well as providing the educational opportunities described on the next page, ultimately each child will take the game home. Before that, pupils can use the letters for ACTIVITY 5.
2. Use a few of the photocopiable examples of category cards (page 23) or make your own e.g. something that you wear; a colour; a vegetable; an animal, an outdoor game, etc. Once the children see how the game works they are very keen to add their own categories and this provides many educational opportunities. Ultimately the children can copy up a few categories of their own to take home.

ACTIVITY 2

To play the game - as a class or large group
1. Put one set of the letters of the alphabet in one container and the categories in another.
2. The game works well if the pupils playing sit in a circle.
3. One person holds both containers and takes out a letter of the alphabet and a category and makes sure he/she can read it. He/she then reads the name of the category and the name of the letter loudly and clearly e.g. "A colour beginning with "r"."
4. The first person to shout out a correct answer gets the paper with the category on.
5. The letter of the alphabet is returned to the box and the letters shuffled a little.
6. The containers are then passed to the next person in the group and the process is repeated.
7. If two people shout an answer at the same time, change the letter of the alphabet.
8. The winner is the person with the most categories.

Notes
It is a good idea to warn the children to shout the answers – the child with the soft voice may get the right answer but may not be heard.

Rule 7. Rather than tell the children what to do when two or three children all give the correct response at the same time, you may want to encourage the children to discuss what could be done, with the final decision being subject to a vote.

A problem that can occur is that "y", "z", "x" and "q" keep turning up, and as there are relatively few words beginning with these letters, they could be removed.

If there is a problem with the pupils reading the categories, the teacher or a pupil volunteer can read all of the categories.

EXTENSION ACTIVITY 1A

Making the alphabet provides a natural opportunity to look at some aspects of the alphabet. This can be extended and developed as appropriate.

Immediate teaching points re: alphabet
1. Knowing all the alphabet in order.
2. The distinction between UPPER and LOWER case.
3. Appreciating that some letters look the same when turned round e.g. in lower case: u/n; p/d; and that some can be confused depending on how they are written e.g. m/w; /u/c; y/h. You may want the children to discover this for themselves when they are playing the game. Similar problems occur with upper case. The children may realise that they will have to make some mark on the paper to show which way up to read the letter.
4. Knowing consonants and vowels; and using the terminology.

Further work re: alphabet
1. Working in pairs, one person shuffles letters of alphabet. The partner puts them back into order. They may like to try beating their own time.
2. When letters of the alphabet are laid out in the correct order, one person removes five letters whilst the partner turns away. The partner then has to see how quickly she/he can work out the missing letters.

EXTENSION ACTIVITY 1B

1) Make sure children can make use of the knowledge of alphabetic order. This can be done using any book, by playing the game: "Open your book as if you are looking up the word "bird"". "Now pretend you are looking up "frog"". Now pretend you are looking up "ant." etc. All the time watch to see that the children are moving backwards and forwards in the book correctly.
2) This might be a time to point out that dictionaries fall into four sectors A-E; F-M; N-S; T-Z. Again children can be asked, for example to look for "monkey", learning to open the book at the half way point. Individual dictionaries for this activity are obviously rewarding.

EXTENSION ACTIVITY 1C

With the letters of the alphabet actually spread out on the desk putting words into alphabetical order becomes far more "real". Put first names of class/group in alphabetical order, first letters only, then perhaps to second letter, etc. Could carry on to surnames, teachers' surnames, names of stores, etc.

EXTENSION ACTIVITY 3A

Designing the box that the game is sold in.

ACTIVITY 4

The poem (Resource sheet 3B)
There is a photocopy of the poem so that pupils can highlight various aspects of the poem in response to some of the questions.

ACTIVITY 5

Making a range of real words by playing with letter order and discussing their meanings before choosing which to use for a poem, will be a stretching activity for many. Some pupils however, with guidance, may be able to take the activity a step further and make non-real words and discuss whether they sound as if they have a meaning, producing finally, as in The Computer's First Christmas Card, a poem containing real and non-real words.

ACTIVITY 7

Resource sheet 3C

The aim of this activity is to give practice in keen observation, accurate description, holding details in the memory for a short time and listening skills. The pupils may be interested to link the activity with the idea of seeing an animal or item they think may be lost and phoning the description to the police or a friend, who may in turn repeat the description to someone else at a later time.

It is important that Pupil 1, doing the describing, does not use arm movements to help the description. Similarly there should be no arm movements when Pupil 2 comes to describe the object. This is to encourage accurate use of language.

When it comes to comparing the two pictures, the teacher ideally needs to see the two pictures first. For example, when one group of three pupils worked on (A) and (a) they thought the picture that Pupil 3 had drawn was the same as (a) in the Teacher's Pack, although Pupil 3 had drawn a lower case "a" rather than the upper case. Pupil 1 had not only not made that distinction but had not realised that the description was capable of being interpreted in a different way and had not noticed the distinction when comparing pictures. Other examples have been that pupils have not noted the fact that two of the A's on the card are upside down, or that the Hearts in the middle are not touching.

Where the two pictures are not identical, and Pupil 3 has not seen the original drawing, then the three children can repeat the process in their original roles, giving the pupil in role 1 a chance to try again. Usually they are very keen to do this until the two pictures are identical.

Where the pupil in role 2 is having difficulty remembering details, she/he could be encouraged to visualise the description.

More templates and details could be made.

EXTENSION ACTIVITY 8A

A group of pupils could be responsible for the wall display.

EXTENSION ACTIVITY 8B

As well as making a wall display, children could send their jokes to various newspapers and magazines. This would give a purpose to writing something out "in best" and addressing envelopes.

Quite a few children may know of comics or magazines that take jokes, and they can bring them in for everyone to see and to contribute to, for example, The Beano.

Resource Sheet 3A Activities 1 & 2

a boy's name	a girl's name
a bird	a colour
an animal	something to wear
a fruit	a vegetable

Resource Sheet 3B Activity 4

"The Computer's First Christmas Card", by Edwin Morgan

jollymerry
hollyberry
jollyberry
merryholly
happyjolly
jollyjelly
bellymerry
hollyheppy
jollyMolly
marryJerry
merryHarry
happyBarry
heppyJarry
boppyheppy
berryjorry
jorryjolly
moppyjelly
Mollymerry
Jerryjolly
bellyboppy
jorryhoppy
hollymoppy
Barrymerry
Jarryhappy
happyboppy
boppyjolly
jollymerry
merrymerry
merrymerry
merryChris
ammerryasa
Chrismerry
asMERRYCHR
YSANTHEMUM

Resource Sheet 3C

Activity 7

A

a

B

b

C

c

UNIT 3 Word Games — Highlight English — 25

UNIT 4 ALL IN A DAY

Further Resources Available

Activity number	Cassette material	Alternative to cassette	Photocopiable material	Alternative to photocopy	Notes
1 and 2			p 28	Pupils could copy-format in PB. p 16	
4			p 28	Text in full, in PB. p 18 + 19	p 27

Analysis of Activities

Statements of Attainment	LEVEL 2						LEVEL 3						SOA'S COVERED		
	a	b	c	d	e	f	a	b	c	d	e	f	Act	SOA	
SPEAKING + LISTENING **1**	2														PB
															TP
READING **2**				4 5						4 5			4,5	4c	PB
															TP
WRITING **3**	3,6	3,6		7			3, 6	3 6		7	3,6		3 6 7	4b 4a 4c	PB
															TP

Key to charts
PB = Pupil's Book   ▓ = Extension activities in TP
TP = Teacher's Pack   SOA = Statement of Attainment

Aims of Unit 4

ACTIVITIES	AIMS
1	To encourage reading with care; to appreciate that diaries often record feelings and thoughts as well as events.
2	To encourage awareness of what people might think and feel about events and to find ways of conveying this in writing.
3	To make a record in diary format of the experiences of an imaginary character using information gained from the first two activities.
4	To encourage careful reading and interpretation of textual clues for prediction purposes.
5	To use the skills gained in activity 4 with the help of a partner.
6	To make decisions about what to write, using the prediction skills gained.
7	To organise thoughts feelings and events into a chart format on an amusing topic.

NOTES ON ACTIVITIES

ACTIVITY 2

Resource Sheet 4A
A photocopiable sheet with blank boxes for pupils to fill in is provided.

ACTIVITY 4

Resource Sheet 4B
This exercise can be done even more effectively by introducing pupils to one section of the story at a time using the cut-up photocopiable page provided.

This anticipation activity which is teacher directed here, is taken up again in Unit 6, Activity 1. The aim is for pupils to apply the skills gained in Unit 4, to a similar activity which they do on their own in Unit 6.

Resource Sheet 4A

Activities 1 & 2

A	B	C
Events/Thoughts	How Chris feels	Details to show how Chris feels

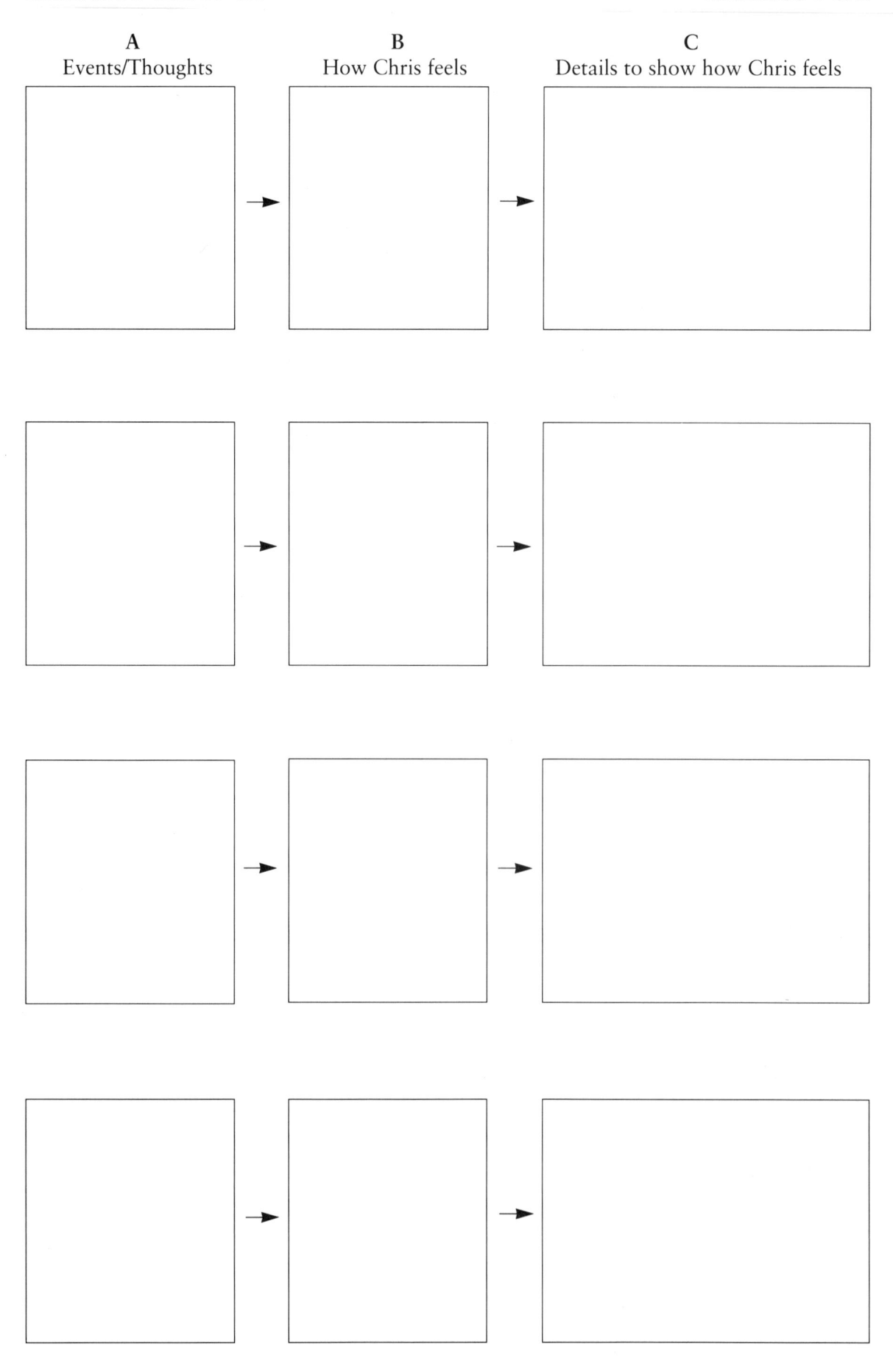

Resource sheet 4B
Activity 4

Curtis looked at the slip of paper and blushed. "Will you come to my disco on Friday?" it said. "It starts at 7.30. Carla." Curtis looked at the note again. There was a small kiss after her name.

Curtis blushed even more. He slipped the paper into his pocket, before Mr Smith spotted it. Then he waited for Carla to turn round.

"Why aren't you working, Curtis Skinner?" Mr Smith asked crossly.
"I am, Sir," Curtis said. "I was just thinking."
"Mmm, well don't strain yourself!" Mr Smith said. One or two of the class giggled. Then Carla turned round and Curtis nodded.
"Curtis!" Mr Smith shouted. "If you haven't done your work by the end of this lesson, you will have to stay in after school."
Curtis bent over his book and tried to work.

"Bring your book up here, Curtis," Mr Smith said, at the end of the lesson.
"It was too hard, Sir," Curtis said, as he put his book on the desk.
"Rubbish!" Mr Smith snapped. "You are one of the best people at maths, in your year! See me in room twenty-six at 3.15."
Curtis opened his mouth to protest, but he knew it was no good.
"What you going to do?" Kevin asked at breaktime. "Your dad won't let you go to the disco, will he?"
"Not if he finds out I'm in detention tonight," Curtis said glumly.

Mr Smith handed Curtis the books. "I'll be back in half an hour," he said.

Curtis sat alone, listening to the clatter of the cleaners. All he could think about was how he get to the disco. He had three days to put his father in the right mood. But how? He could get the dinner ready at night and lay the table. But he did that most nights anyway. What else could he do?
Suddenly Curtis heard footsteps and the door was flung open.

"What's this?" Mr Smith said, when he looked at the books. "You've been here all this time and done nothing!"
For a moment Curtis thought Mr Smith was going to burst. Then he seemed to calm down. "Anything wrong at home?" he asked suddenly, peering closely at Curtis.
Curtis shook his head.
"Right then." Mr Smith said, coldly. "Bring me this work at ten to nine, tomorrow. And do two extra pages. If you don't. I'll write to your father."

UNIT 5 A PANTOMIME - WRITING FOR CHILDREN

Further Resources Available

Activity number	Cassette material	Alternative to cassette	Photocopiable material	Alternative to photocopy	Notes
1	Pantomime	Pupils and teacher could read	p 34	Script included for convenience and furtherwork Not essential	p 32
4	Pantomime	Pupils and teacher could read	p 36		p 32
7					p 32

Analysis of Activities

Statements of Attainment	LEVEL 2 a	b	c	d	e	f	LEVEL 3 a	b	c	d	e	f	SOA'S COVERED Act	SOA
SPEAKING + LISTENING **1**	6		1, 3, 4, 6											PB
	6A 7E	7D					7D	7E						TP
READING **2**					1, 3, 4				1, 3		1, 3, 4	4c	PB
	1A													TP
WRITING **3**	5				5							7		PB
	7C 7F 7G	7C	7F 7G	7A			7B 7E 7F 7G	7C 7G 7F	7B 7G 7F	7A	7C 7G 7F	7A,7B 7F 7G	4c 4a 4b	TP

Key to charts
PB = Pupil's Book   ▒ = Extension activities in TP
TP = Teacher's Pack   SOA = Statement of Attainment

Aims of Unit 5

ACTIVITIES	AIMS
1	To enjoy listening to and gain experience of a play for younger children; to encourage careful listening, using clues in the script and knowledge of what amuses younger children, to predict the plot; to encourage careful reading and experience of the play format.
1A	To learn some of the skills of reading a play script; to encourage pupils to use their voices to convey meaning and portray a character.
2	To encourage careful reading; to extend awareness that scripts for stage include not only what characters say, but information about what they do and the manner in which they do it.
3	To encourage pupils to think about the appropriateness of a play for its intended audience.
4	To provide enjoyment and greater understanding of how plots and characters are developed during the course of a complete act in a play.
5	To develop the ability to collate information about and interpret the behaviour of a character and in the process learn some of the skills of writing a character sketch.
6	To use the knowledge gained about a play, characters in the play and writing for a specific audience, to plan the content of another act for the play.
6A	To help develop ideas for a scene in the play in a situation which focuses on speech and behaviour and in the process to heighten awareness of audience, character and plot.
7	To use the knowledge gained in the previous activities to experience putting ideas into play format.
7A	To practise presentation skills by designing a poster for the pantomime.
7B & 7C	To think about the plot and characters of the pantomime more closely by writing a review and/or the main character's diary.
7D & 7E	To turn the story of the pantomime into a different form of story which could be told to younger children. To extend imagination by inventing new characters and incorporating them into an oral story.
7F & 7G	To study the conventions of books produced for young children and then try writing one, drawing on the stories compiled in previous activities.

NOTES ON ACTIVITIES

ACTIVITY 1

Cassette (Resource Sheet 5A)
Although the whole of ACT TWO of the pantomime is on tape, the idea is to use it in three parts:
i) From the beginning of ACT TWO to the point where the script is transcribed into the Pupil's Book. The pupils then discuss what they think is going to happen next. They can then read the transcript in the Pupil's Book to see to what extent their predictions were right.
ii) The part that is transcribed in the Pupil's Book only. This is included for a number of reasons e.g. in case teachers would rather the children listened to the tape to check their predictions rather than go straight into the manuscript, or vice versa or for other purposes. (See Ext. Activity 1A below)
iii) From the end of the transcript in the Pupil's Book to the end of that part of the tape. (Activity 4)

EXTENSION ACTIVITY 1A

Where appropriate, pupils could work in pairs to practise reading the script aloud, working out just how the lines would be said, what sort of pauses there would be, etc. They could then hear the tape of this part of the play and discuss what they have learnt about reading a script. Pupils could then try reading the manuscript again using some of the ideas discussed.

ACTIVITY 4

Resource Sheet 5A
The whole transcript of the play extract on cassette is included, with the aim of making it easier, amongst other things, to anticipate points where the tape might be stopped in order to ask the pupils questions.

EXTENSION ACTIVITY 6A

If role play is feasible, pupils could work in groups, and use the details in Activity 6 as a start to role play, finishing when the princess is rescued and Beadle dispatched.

ACTIVITY 7

The piece of script from the pantomime is given here as a model for setting out plays for the theatre.

EXTENSION ACTIVITY 7A

Design a programme or poster for the pantomime in the unit.

EXTENSION ACTIVITY 7B

Write a review of the pantomime.

EXTENSION ACTIVITY 7C

Write John Tully's diary recording the experiences or some of the experiences he had in ACT 2.

EXTENSION ACTIVITY 7D

Children could tell the story of John Tully and the Fizzwhizz, trying to recount it so that it would be of interest to a younger audience. This could be done with children taking it in turns to tell a part of the story.

EXTENSION ACTIVITY 7E

The idea of an imaginary animal could be extended. Children could make up their own animals. This could be done by drawing a doodle, and giving it eyes, etc. and a name.

Children could think up a scenario, e.g. where it lives and what it does, what kind of creature it is — building on the character sketch they did of a Fizzwhizz. They could plan what sort of adventures it might get up to.

EXTENSION ACTIVITY 7F

A part of the pantomime could be changed into a book for younger children. This activity could be prefaced by the class looking at younger children's books with the aim of seeing how much text there is in relation to illustrations, etc.

EXTENSION ACTIVITY 7G

Pupils could then write a book for younger children, using the activities in 7E, working alone, in pairs or in a small group, with each taking on a specific role; the degree of teacher involvement depending on the abilities of the pupils.

It might be possible to match with a similar group from a primary school, so that books are written for specific children.

Resource Sheet 5A　　　　　　　　　　　　　　　　　　　　　　　Activities 1 + 4

THE PANTOMIME

JOHN TULLY　　You do know where we are going to, don't you?
HUMBLE　　　　Oh yes; at least, I know the general direction ... more or less

(JOHN TULLY looks sceptical.)

　　　　　　　　I'm not lost

JOHN TULLY　　Let's hope you're not, because I am. I've never felt so far from home in all my life. I'll tell you another thin, too – I'm hungry.

HUMBLE　　　　Why didn't you say so? I have some food.
JOHN TULLY　　Have you? What?
HUMBLE　　　　Just a minute.

(HUMBLE takes a package, wrapped in cloth, out of his pocket.)

　　　　　　　　Here. Have that.

JOHN TULLY　　(Unwrapping it) What is it?
HUMBLE　　　　Pollen bread with honey on it.
JOHN TULLY　　Oh, very nice.

(He sits on a mossy stone, and starts eating.)

　　　　　　　　Aren't you having any?
HUMBLE　　　　Er ... No, I don't think so.
JOHN TULLY　　Have half?
HUMBLE　　　　No, I'll tell you what I'll do – those flowers we passed a short way back – I can get honey and pollen from them.
JOHN TULLY　　Hey, you're not leaving me, are you?
HUMBLE　　　　I won't be long.
JOHN TULLY　　Don't forget where I am, will you?
HUMBLE　　　　I won't. (He turns away and back.) Oh, there's just one thing. If you see a Fizzwhizz, don't pay any attention to it.
JOHN TULLY　　A Fizzwhizz?
HUMBLE　　　　Yes; it's just a nuisance. It may be attracted by the honey, but don't give it any – it will only encourage it. It will go away if you ignore it. All right?
JOHN TULLY　　Aye, I think so.
HUMBLE　　　　I'll be as quick as I can.
　　　　　　　　(Humble goes out.)

(i) STOP THE TAPE.

34 ──────────── Highlight English ──────────── UNIT 5 A Pantomime – Writing for Children

(ii) START THE TAPE.

JOHN TULLY (Eating) If it wants any of this it will have to be sharp. Oh I am hungry.

(Slowly, a FIZZWHIZZ head appears from the wings, makes a cuckoo noise and disappears.)

FIZZWHIZZ Cuckoo.
JOHN TULLY (Puzzled) Funny ...

(The FIZZWHIZZ appears from the other side and vanishes.)

FIZZWHIZZ Cuckoo.
JOHN TULLY Very funny

(A FIZZWHIZZ head appears upside down, from the wings.)

FIZZWHIZZ Cuckoo.
JOHN TULLY (Still eating) It'll be a Fizzwhizz. I'll just ignore it.)

(The FIZZWHIZZ) patters across the stage.)
FIZZWHIZZ Cuckoo. Cuckoo.
JOHN TULLY I'm not going to look at it. I'm having nothing to do with it.

(The FIZZWHIZZ hops round JOHN TULLY then sits at his feet.)

FIZZWHIZZ Hello. I'm the Fizzwhizz.
JOHN TULLY (Not looking at it) I know. Go away. I don't want you.
FIZZWHIZZ All right. I'll go.

(The FIZZWHIZZ starts going away quickly.)

JOHN TULLY There you are. You just have to be firm with them.
FIZZWHIZZ (From off stage) I've gone!
FIZZWHIZZ (From further away) I've gone!
FIZZWHIZZ (Very loudly, over the loud speakers) I'VE GONE!
JOHN TULLY Oh, I wish it would leave me alone.

(The FIZZWHIZZ patters back and sits at JOHN TULLY'S feet.)

FIZZWHIZZ (Sweetly) I'm the Fizzwhizz.
JOHN TULLY I know you're the Fizzwhizz. I can see you're the Fizzwhizz but I don't want you around. Go AWAY!
FIZZWHIZZ (Bursting into tears and howling) Wah-wah-wah-wah.
JOHN TULLY Oh dear. I'm sorry I didn't mean...
FIZZWHIZZ Wah-wah-wah-wah.
JOHN TULLY Oh dear. Don't get upset. Look. Have this bread and honey.

(The FIZZWHIZZ stops crying, grabs the sandwich and starts eating happily.)

(ii) STOP THE TAPE.
(iii) START THE TAPE.

JOHN TULLY   Well, I don't know. All that for a honey butty.
(The FIZZWHIZZ starts to move off.)

You going now?

(The FIZZWHIZZ nods.)

You're not coming back?

(The FIZZWHIZZ shakes its head.)

Thank goodness for that.

(The Fizzwhizz waves its free hand.)

Ta-ra.

FIZZWHIZZ   (Happily) I'm the Fizzwhizz.
JOHN TULLY   Yes, that's right. Ta-ra.

(The FIZZWHIZZ goes off.)

Whew! What a carry on.

(HUMBLE re-enters, closely followed, in step by the FIZZWHIZZ. JOHN TULLY turns and sees them.)

JOHN TULLY	GET OUT!
HUMBLE	I beg your pardon?
JOHN TULLY	Not you – that Fizzwhizz.
HUMBLE	(Turning round) Fizzwhizz? Where?
JOHN TULLY	It was following you. But it's gone now. Come on, before it comes back.
HUMBLE	Why, has it been bothering you?
JOHN TULLY	It's been a flaming pest.
HUMBLE	You didn't give it anything did you?
JOHN TULLY	I gave it a bit of my sandwich to get rid of it.
HUMBLE	No! You'll never get rid of it now. It will follow you everywhere.
JOHN TULLY	How did I know? You never told me that.
HUMBLE	I did. I told you not to give it anything.
JOHN TULLY	Oh, well, I've done it now. Come on, we'd better get going.
HUMBLE	Wait. I think we'd better decide what's the best thing to do.
JOHN TULLY	You are lost, aren't you?
HUMBLE	Well ...

JOHN TULLY	Aren't you?
HUMBLE	Yes, I am.
JOHN TULLY	I thought so.
HUMBLE	I really don't know the way at all.

(The FIZZWHIZZ appears.)

FIZZWHIZZ	I know.
JOHN TULLY	Go away!
FIZZWHIZZ	All right.

(It goes off.)

JOHN TULLY	Pest! – Hey, I wonder if it does?
HUMBLE	Of course it doesn't. It's merely being a nuisance.
JOHN TULLY	How do you know it doesn't?
HUMBLE	Because it's utterly brainless, that's why.
JOHN TULLY	Well, it's not lost, anyroad. – Hey! Come here!
FIZZWHIZZ	(Entering) Yes?
JOHN TULLY	Now, just listen a minute –
FIZZWHIZZ	I'm the Fizzwhizz.
JOHN TULLY	Yes, I know. We want to get to the Paper Palace.
FIZZWHIZZ	Paper Palace?
JOHN TULLY	Yes.
FIZZWHIZZ	It's perfectly possible to proceed to the Paper Palace.
JOHN TULLY	How do we get there then?
FIZZWHIZZ	I'm the Fizzwhizz.
JOHN TULLY	All right! Now which way is it?
FIZZWHIZZ	The Paper Palace.
JOHN TULLY	Right.
FIZZWHIZZ	No, left. Follow me. (Sets off.) Hold tight. Ding-ding. Mind the doors please. Woo-Wooh!

(It patters round the stage and off.)

HUMBLE	There you are, you see. It's perfectly brainless, and it doesn't know anything.
FIZZWHIZZ	(Re-appearing) I do too. This way please. Mind the step. Oops! (It goes off.)
JOHN TULLY	I think it does know. You can please yourself, but I'm going after it.
FIZZWHIZZ	(Re-entering) Flight 525 at 0.55 now leaving from Gate 5. Fasten your seat-belts. (Goes off.)
JOHN TULLY	Are you coming or not?
HUMBLE	I have a feeling we shall live to regret this.

(HUMBLE follows JOHN TULLY off.)

UNIT 6 WORK IT OUT

Further Resources Available

Activity number	Cassette material	Alternative to cassette	Photocopiable material	Alternative to photocopy	Notes
1					p 39
2			p 41, 42	Everything in PB but small	p 40

Analysis of Activities

Statements of Attainment	LEVEL 2 a	b	c	d	e	f	LEVEL 3 a	b	c	d	e	f	SOA'S COVERED Act	SOA	
SPEAKING + LISTENING **1**									2				2	4d	PB
															TP
READING **2**							1	1		1			1	4a 4c	PB
															TP
WRITING **3**															PB
															TP

Key to charts
PB = Pupil's Book   ▓ = Extension activities in TP
TP = Teacher's Pack   SOA = Statement of Attainment

Aims of Unit 6

ACTIVITIES	AIMS
1	To encourage careful reading and interpretation of textual clues to place a range of texts into a wider context.
2	To widen the range of reading material and in the process discover the type of information recorded on tickets of various sorts in a problem solving situation requiring collaboration.
2A	To develop understanding of the kind of information recorded on different tickets and receipts.

Notes on Activities

ACTIVITY 1

Answers

A BEFORE
Ray had removed the mirror from the dressing table. Gary had locked the door. The answer could include the fact that Ray or both of the boys had hunted for and found two snails or that the snails were pets and they had collected them from where they were kept. Also, some cabbage had been obtained.

AFTER
There will be a snail "race".

B BEFORE
The man had been to a graveyard and removed a ring from the finger of a skeleton.

AFTER
The skeleton takes the ring from the woman or the woman in her terror throws the ring to it or the woman runs away in fear, chased by the skeleton or a similar ending suggesting that the skeleton goes to any lengths to get the ring.

C BEFORE
Two cards, the nine of Clubs and the Jack of Spades have been soaked in (warm) water. When thoroughly wet the back has been peeled away from the front of both cards which have then been laid out to dry. Other answers could be added to this, such as the reader was asked to obtain a pack of cards, glue and a bowl of water.

AFTER
An acceptable answer would make the point that the conjuror establishes that she/he can change the nine of Clubs to the Jack of Spades and then does so by passing a hand (or handkerchief or similar) in front of the card and then dropping the flap to reveal the Jack of Spades; or the answer could be that to do the trick, the conjuror will need a lot of practice, learning to drop the flap at the same time as passing the other hand in front of the card (or similar). The answer could state that the conjuror could use a magic word or magic wand to make it look as if the properties of these were responsible for the transformation.

D BEFORE

The boy in the story has done a pile of washing up and the plates have been stacked; he has been moaning whilst washing up; the washing up has not been perfect as there is still a bit of food on one of the plates. The boy had offered to do the washing up in the first place but had hoped that the offer wouldn't be accepted.

AFTER

In the process of extricating the bottom plate from the stack, the whole stack will topple over and probably crash down and smash on to the floor. Gran will be livid.

ACTIVITY 2

Resource Sheets 6A

The clues provided in the Pupil's Book are also given in a larger size on the photocopiable sheets provided.

Answers

1. The journey Laura made was:
   A bus journey from Warden to Hexham and a train journey from Hexham to the Metrocentre near Gateshead or Newcastle. D was used for the bus journey to Hexham.

2. The person who wrote the letter probably lives in or near Gateshead as there was not a great deal of time after the cinema for Laura to get to the house. Laura was probably the sister or the sister-in-law of the girl who wrote the letter, as the girl says her daughter calls Laura "Aunty".

3. Laura's movements are as follows.
   (i) From Warden to Hexham by bus; Warden is the supposed starting point in the light of the address on the envelope.
   (ii) Shopping in Hexham as evidenced by the receipt from the Pop Shop with the time stamp: 10.30 am.
   (iii) By train from Hexham to Gateshead (the Metrocentre); evidence: rail ticket.
   (iv) At the cinema at the Metrocentre, time: 1.30; evidence: cinema ticket.
   (v) To sister's or sister-in-law's house to arrive at five o'clock or a bit later; supposition based on part of the letter sent by the sister/sister-in-law, which stated there would be someone at home after 5 o'clock.

EXTENSION ACTIVITY 2A

Children could be encouraged to bring in all kinds of receipts and tickets to see what kinds of information is on them and how they compare with the ones in the Pupil's Book.

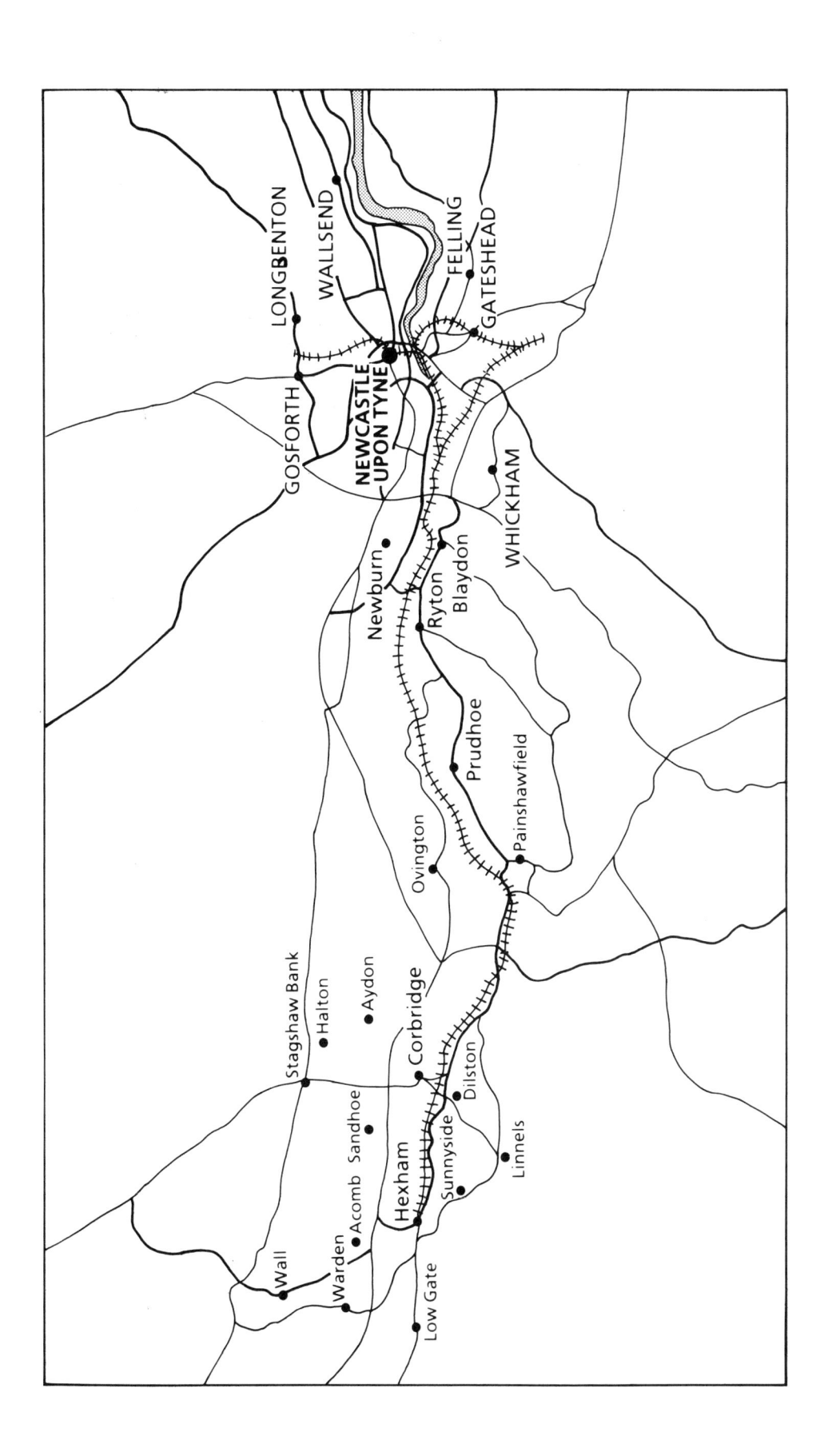

Resource Sheet 6A

Activity 2

Resource Sheet 6A
Activity 2

A

```
   POPSHOP
   HEXHAM
VAT No 194 2952 34
    14-03-92

TO-BCAT      8.45
TOTAL        8.45
CATEND       9.00

ITEM    1
CLERK 2 9688 10:30TM
```

B

```
Class   Ticket type        Adult   Child
STD  CHEAPDY RTN CD     ONE    NIL     RTN

           Date         Number
        14 MAR 92       89335    3207@4731W02
From                    Valid            Price
HEXHAM              * AS ADVERTISED      £ 4·50
To                      Route
METROCENTRE     *                        0849

         British Rail
```

C

```
uci  MORE CHOICE OF MORE  22103240   uci       22103240
     MOVIES IN MORE COMFORT

  1    9    12          TICKET         TICKET   METROCE
                                                GATESHD
  METROCENTR      SAT  14-3-92  1-30  3·00  14-3-92  1-30  3·00
  GATESHEAD
```

D

```
050 -21 9 06
```

E

Laura Cheung.
Slip Cottage.
Warden,
Northumberland

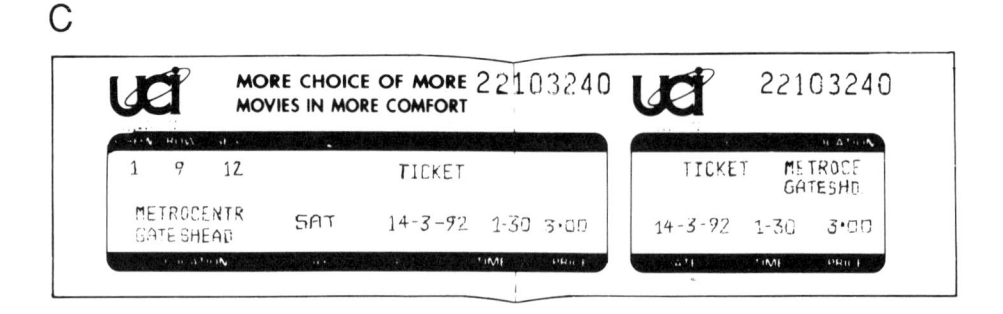

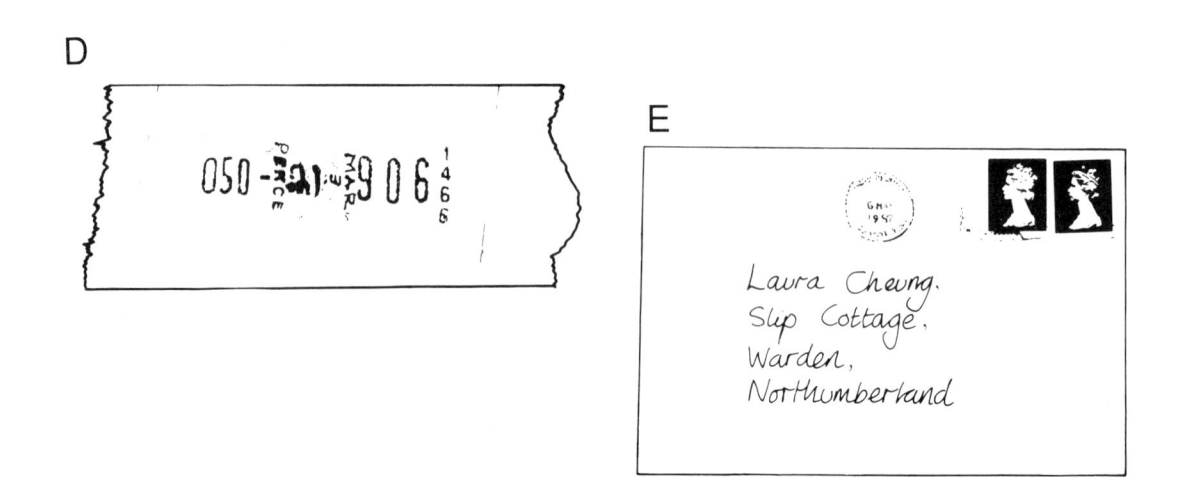

F

Can't wait to see you. Don't forget
we won't be back until five.
         Love
              Camille
P.S. Stephanie calls you Aunty Aura!

UNIT 7 VIEWS, VIEWS, VIEWS

Further Resources Available

Activity number	Cassette material	Alternative to cassette	Photocopiable material	Alternative to photocopy	Notes
5A					p 44
8A					p 44

Analysis of Activities

Statements of Attainment		LEVEL 2 a	b	c	d	e	f	LEVEL 3 a	b	c	d	e	f	SOA'S COVERED Act	SOA	
SPEAKING + LISTENING	**1**		7							7				5 7	5d 4c	PB
																TP
READING	**2**															PB
														5A	5b	TP
WRITING	**3**	4 8						4 8	4	8	3	4 8		3 8	4c 4c	PB
		5A 8A						5A 8A		5A 8A	5A 8A			5A 8A	4c 4c	TP

Key to charts
PB = Pupil's Book   ▓ = Extension activities in TP
TP = Teacher's Pack   SOA = Statement of Attainment

Aims of Unit 7

ACTIVITIES	AIMS
1	To encourage careful reading of a type of article often found in television magazines and to look at someone's reasons for having particular preferences.
2	To focus on a writing skill with the aim of encouraging children to emulate it in their own writing and be aware of it in other people's writing.
3	To encourage pupils to think about the reasons why they like or dislike something in preparation for writing their own article.
4	To give experience of ordering ideas and putting views and opinions into writing.
5	To give experience of the format and conventions associated with a letters page in a popular children's magazine.
5A	To encourage interest in reading children's magazines; to provide ideas for the pupils to write, draw, present and organise lively and amusing material and so become familiar with some of the conventions and formats found in children's magazines.
6	To encourage reading with care and so focus on views held about the effects of some television programmes on audiences.
7	To encourage pupils to consider the programmes they watch in the light of a range of audiences.
8	To express opinions in writing; to gain experience of writing a letter with a real purpose and to a known source.
8A	To provide the opportunity for pupils to organise ideas into logical sequences using subject matter with which they are very familiar; where appropriate learn some of the higher order skills.

NOTES ON ACTIVITIES

EXTENSION ACTIVITY 5A

Looking at the letters page of Fast Forward may stimulate interest in comics and magazines and could provide the occasion for children to bring in magazines for groups/the class to look at. Depending on ability, some pupils could produce a class comic or pages from a comic. For example, Look-in at the moment, includes a colourful double spread at the back with a good variety of short items of the sort which children would enjoy writing for themselves.

EXTENSION ACTIVITY 8A

If interest still runs high on the subject of television, children could write about what happens in their favourite programme, with the aim of explaining the programme for someone who has never seen it.

This can be made as hard or as simple as required. For example, the description of a games show may need considerable organisation and this could provide the opportunity to look at methods of tackling this type of activity. e.g. jotting down in rough all the aspects of the game show and then putting them into order and organising them afterwards.

Instead or in addition, pupils can describe or make a cartoon strip of their favourite soap, series or film with the aim of giving details in chronological order. Where it is a film or series everyone in the group watches, children could take it in turns to give the details.

UNIT 8 FAIR PLAY

Further Resources Available

Activity number	Cassette material	Alternative to cassette	Photocopiable material	Alternative to photocopy	Notes
1,2,3,4					p 46
3	Sound effects				p 46

Analysis of Activities

Statements of Attainment	LEVEL 2 a	b	c	d	e	f	LEVEL 3 a	b	c	d	e	f	SOA'S COVERED Act	SOA	
SPEAKING + LISTENING **1**	9								9				10	4c	PB
															TP
READING **2**							7	7		7			8	4c	PB
															TP
WRITING **3**	5						5	5	5		5				PB
															TP

Key to charts
PB = Pupil's Book   ▓ = Extension activities in TP
TP = Teacher's Pack   SOA = Statement of Attainment

Aims of Unit 8

ACTIVITIES	AIMS
1	To gather a small list of nouns associated with fairs, in preparation for a piece of intensive description.
2	To encourage pupils to explore ways of looking at and describing objects; to deepen understanding of how the choice of vocabulary adds to meaning.
3	To gather a small list of words associated with fairs and in the process to give practice in listening carefully and identifying and interpreting a range of sounds.
4	To encourage pupils to develop understanding of how choice of vocabulary extends meaning.
5	To use the notes made in the previous activities to capture the atmosphere and activities of a familiar scene.
6	To encourage pupils to think about the meanings of words and how meanings can be conveyed graphically.
7	To encourage reading with care, focusing on the structural links in and between sentences.
8	To encourage careful reading and extend understanding by anticipating behaviour of characters from a text.
9	To provide the opportunity for pupils to discuss opinions and feelings and describe experiences on a controversial topic.
10	To practise expressing opinions and feelings succinctly and with clarity; to widen the audience for a presentation; to give experience and heighten awareness of some of the ways a radio programme is put together.

NOTES ON ACTIVITIES

ACTIVITIES 1, 2, 3 and 4

This could be an appropriate time to introduce grammatical terms such as noun and adjective and possibly verb.

ACTIVITY 3

The sounds which can be heard on the tape are:
1) Man calling from Hot Dog stand; 2) Rifle shots; 3) Woman screaming on ride;
4) Man calling 3 goes 25p; 5) Ghost train: doors banging, laughter, train noises;
6) People laughing in the Hall of Mirrors.
A general background noise of fairground music and laughter continues throughout.

UNIT 9 IN THE NEWS

Further Resources Available

Activity number	Cassette material	Alternative to cassette	Photocopiable material	Alternative to photocopy	Notes
6,7,8			p 49 + 50	Most in PB. 3 extra in photocopy.	p 48

Analysis of Activities

Statements of Attainment	LEVEL 2						LEVEL 3						SOA'S COVERED	
	a	b	c	d	e	f	a	b	c	d	e	f	Act	SOA
SPEAKING + LISTENING 1	3	3					3							PB
														TP
READING 2													6,7,8	4c	PB
														TP
WRITING 3	4			2			4		2	4	4		2 4 4 4	4c 4e 4a 4c	PB
														TP

Key to charts
PB = Pupil's Book   = Extension activities in TP
TP = Teacher's Pack   SOA = Statement of Attainment

Aims of Unit 9

ACTIVITIES	AIMS
1	To encourage reading with care and give experience of a well-known format found in newspapers for children and adults.
2	To encourage reading with understanding by transposing information from the article into a different format; to gain experience of ordering information and making decisions to maximise effect, for a specific purpose and audience.
3	To stimulate discussion and exchange of ideas and anecdotes.
4	To give experience of ordering ideas and expressing information in a newspaper format and in the process heighten understanding of the format.
5	To encourage interest in some of the ways of presenting articles, headlines and photographs.
6	To give experience of some of the conventions of headlines; to build on and extend understanding of puns; to encourage careful reading.
7	To encourage careful reading and extend experience of material from a newspaper in an amusing and problem solving way.
8	To further understanding of the language and conventions of newspaper headlines and articles.

NOTES ON ACTIVITIES

ACTIVITIES 6, 7 and 8

Photocopying (Resource Sheet 9A)
The photocopies include 3 extra headlines and 3 extra extracts if a more difficult activity than the one in the Pupil's Book is required.
  The headlines and extracts from articles match in the following way:
A = 2
B = 6
C = 1
D = 5
E = 4
F = 3
G = 7

Extra headlines and extracts
H = 10
I = 9
J = 8

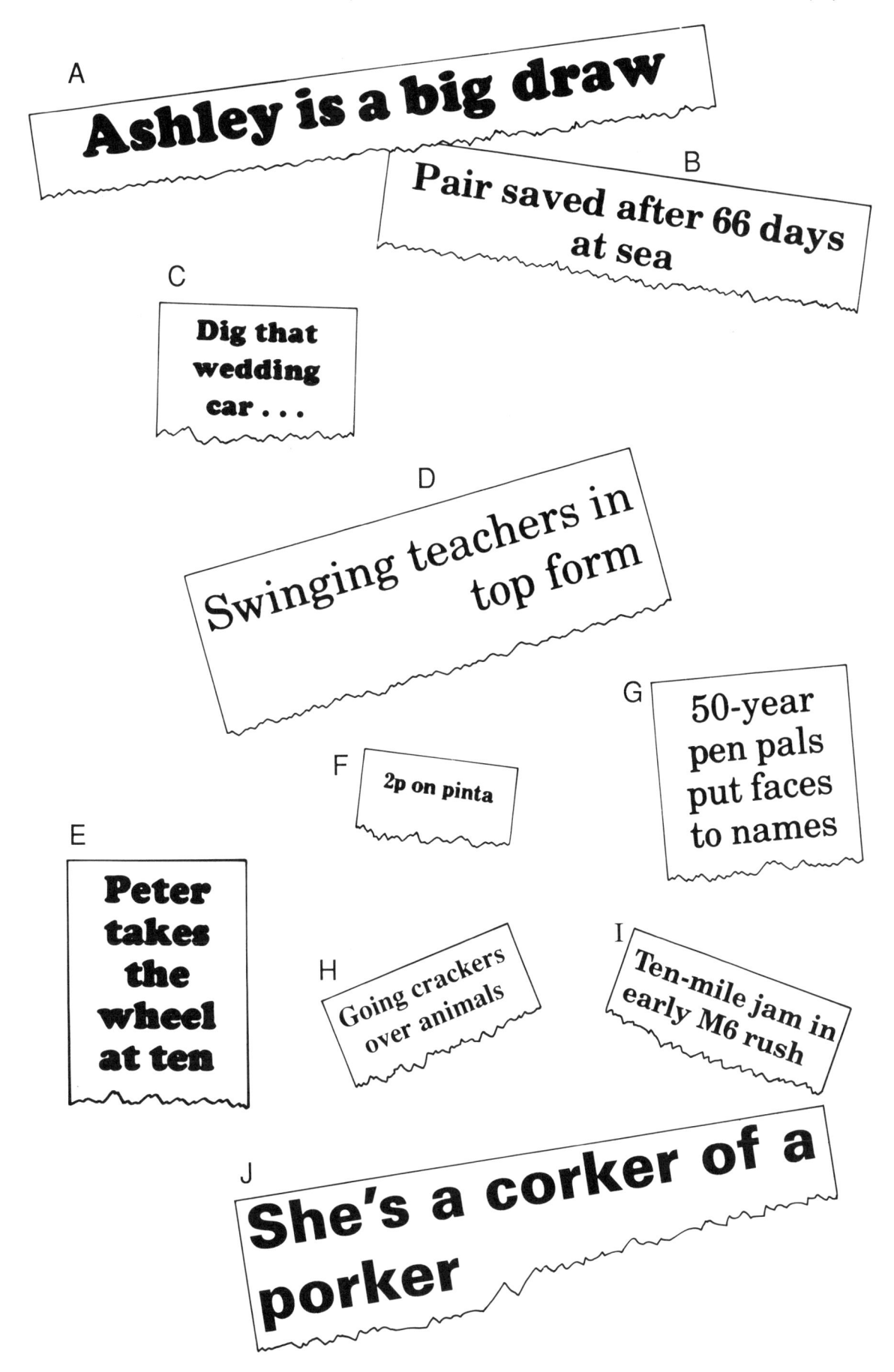

Resource Sheet 9A Activities 6, 7, + 8

A **Ashley is a big draw**

B Pair saved after 66 days at sea

C **Dig that wedding car...**

D Swinging teachers in top form

G 50-year pen pals put faces to names

F 2p on pinta

E **Peter takes the wheel at ten**

H Going crackers over animals

I Ten-mile jam in early M6 rush

J **She's a corker of a porker**

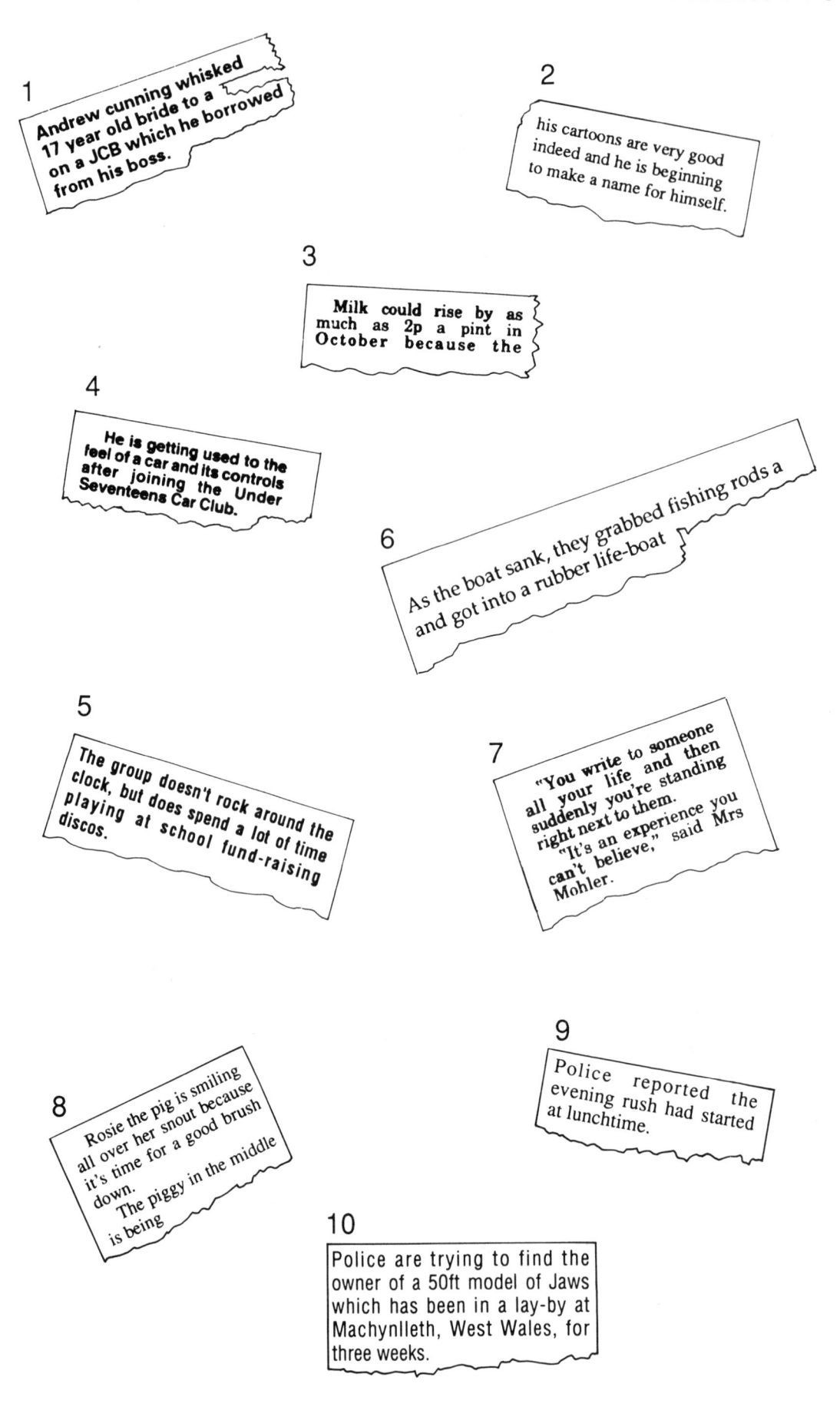

Resource Sheet 9A

Activities 7 + 8

1 Andrew cunning whisked 17 year old bride to a on a JCB which he borrowed from his boss.

2 his cartoons are very good indeed and he is beginning to make a name for himself.

3 Milk could rise by as much as 2p a pint in October because the

4 He is getting used to the feel of a car and its controls after joining the Under Seventeens Car Club.

5 The group doesn't rock around the clock, but does spend a lot of time playing at school fund-raising discos.

6 As the boat sank, they grabbed fishing rods a and got into a rubber life-boat

7 "You write to someone all your life and then suddenly you're standing right next to them. "It's an experience you can't believe," said Mrs Mohler.

8 Rosie the pig is smiling all over her snout because it's time for a good brush down.
The piggy in the middle is being

9 Police reported the evening rush had started at lunchtime.

10 Police are trying to find the owner of a 50ft model of Jaws which has been in a lay-by at Machynlleth, West Wales, for three weeks.

UNIT 10 SCHOOL DAYS

Further Resources Available

Activity number	Cassette material	Alternative to cassette	Photocopiable material	Alternative to photocopy	Notes
1	Story	Could be read by teacher.	p 55-58	Transcript of story provided for teacher reference.	p 53
7					p 54
8					p 54

Analysis of Activities

Statements of Attainment	LEVEL 2 a	b	c	d	e	f	LEVEL 3 a	b	c	d	e	f	SOA'S COVERED Act	SOA	
SPEAKING + LISTENING (1)															PB
	3A	3A		3D				3A		3D					TP
READING (2)	2	2		1	1			1		1, 2, 3	1		8, 9	5e	PB
															TP
WRITING (3)	5 6		6				5 6	6	6	5 7	6		6	4a	PB
				3B 3C						3B 3C					TP

Key to charts
PB = Pupil's Book ▨ = Extension activities in TP
TP = Teacher's Pack SOA = Statement of Attainment

Aims of Unit 10

ACTIVITIES	AIMS
1	To help pupils enjoy listening to a short story and in the process develop an understanding of the motives and feelings of the main characters.
2	To further understanding of the story.
3	To further understanding of the motives, feelings and behaviour of the main characters in the story.
3A	To encourage pupils to look at their own experiences and stimulate discussion in preparation for writing their own short stories.
3B	To encourage pupils to make decisions about selecting information; to become familiar with putting information into a question and answer format.
3C	To encourage visualisation and clear expression in a visual format of the spatial relationships of features of a familiar area.
3D	To encourage visualisation and clear verbal expression of the spatial relationships of features of a familiar area; to encourage careful listening.
4	To listen for specific information; to collect details in note form.
5	To collate details for a character sketch and in the process gain experience of supporting views with appropriate evidence.
6	To experience writing about personal experiences using the information and skills gained in the previous activities.
6A	To encourage interest in and awareness of some aspects of books.
7	To promote interest in book covers and in the process gain understanding of some of the aims and functions of a cover.
8	To encourage reading with care; discussion about choice of words.
9	To explore the effects of different choices of words and in the process deepen understanding of a poem.

NOTES ON ACTIVITIES

ACTIVITY 1

Resource Sheets 10A

Listening to the story and stopping for discussion may well take a full period or double period. For this reason ACTIVITIES 2 and 3 provide the chance to check memory, the text helping to act as a reminder. Having answered the questions in ACTIVITY 2 orally, ACTIVITY 3 provides the opportunity for children to apply the skills gained with a written response. A full transcript is provided with suggestions about where discussion stops might be made.

EXTENSION ACTIVITY 3A

At some point, particularly before pupils write their own short story, there could be a discussion about what it is like to start at a new school. This could provide opportunities for the pupils to relate their experiences and for the rest of the group to listen, add to the discussion, reply to the points made, etc. depending upon the group.

Discussion points could include: early school memories; starting a new school because of a family move; first experiences when pupils joined their present school. Another talking point that might arise could be what pupils were told about their present school before they came and how this compared with what it was like when they arrived.

EXTENSION ACTIVITY 3B

The points raised in the discussions could be turned into a question and answer pamphlet suitable for a prospective pupil.

EXTENSION ACTIVITY 3C

Prepare a map of lower school for the pupils to use on the first few days at school. The degree of detail will vary according to abilities.

EXTENSION ACTIVITY 3D

1 Children could practise giving instructions about how to reach various parts of the school. This could be graded. Initially locations can be picked that are two instructions away e.g. Go out of this door and turn right and room 22 is the first door on the left.
2 This could be extended by asking pupils to imagine they are away from the immediate reference point and in some other area of the school. Pupils could be asked to give instructions to various places from there.
3 An extension of this which would need some pre-planning is for the children to work in pairs: A and B. The teacher tells A the location to send B. A then gives the instructions to B (without revealing the destination). B follows the instructions and then comes back to say where the destination was.

EXTENSION ACTIVITY 6A

Looking at book covers and first pages.

This could be a good time to pick a range of books suitable for the pupils to find out what is on a cover, fly leaf, first pages, etc. The amount covered in this activity and the organisation chosen depends on the abilities of the children. For example, this could be an investigative activity, with the children working in groups. One aspect could be taken at a time e.g. finding out what information is on the front cover. After five minutes or so the groups could come together to discuss what they have found out.

Possible teaching points

A Front cover: title, name of author, illustration, possibly publisher. Discussion points: how much a cover encourages/discourages looking at the book in more detail; the sort of bookcover liked best (photo/drawing); how much the title matters; the different publishers represented in the books being looked at; what publishers do.

B Back cover; write up, UK price, ISBN number, bar code. Discussion points: what UK means; what the ISBN number is and why it is needed; bar code, how it works, how is it helpful, where else bar codes found.

Note ISBN stands for International Standard Book Number.
It is composed of a code for the publisher (first string of numbers), a code for the book itself (second string) and a computer check digit (last number). The number for each book is a unique identifier which prevents it being confused with other books with the same or similar titles, author names, publisher names, etc.

C Other pages: dedication, when book first published, other printings, copyright. Discussion points: why authors might dedicate their book to someone and who they might choose; why reprintings are necessary, which books are reprinted; what copyright means, why it is necessary.

D This might be a good time to discuss how to choose a reading book.

ACTIVITY 7

Pupils may need to be reminded that when they come to write a few sentences about the title story, the purpose of the activity is to inform the reader in general terms without giving too much away and spoiling the story.

ACTIVITY 8

Answers to cloze
1 = doubled   2 = frozen   3 = ache   4 = balances
5 = fumble   6 = numb   7 = white

Resource Sheet 10A   Activity 1

The Big Red Apple

I was only half asleep when Grandma came in to wake me up. "Come on. Come on! Show a leg. Up you get. It's that new school today so get in the kitchen and have a good wash."

She'd laid out my new clothes on the chair: new grey shorts, new grey shirt, new grey pullover with two blue stripes around the neck and the cuffs, new grey socks with blue stripes to match, new black shoes that had already been cleaned twice, although I'd only worn them once, and my cousin's old black blazer that he'd grown out of. The clothes were stiff and itchy, the shirt collar hurt straight away, and the shoes were hard and creaky. It took ages to put the clothes on, all the button holes were tight and the tie wouldn't tie properly.

When I got downstairs, Grandma was flapping about trying to find some coins for the dinner money. She looked at me. "Whatever have you done with them clothes? You look like a rag and bone man. And that hair!"
She made me stand still while she tied my tie and folded the itchy collar down and tucked my shirt into my trousers properly. Then she sorted my hair out by spitting on a brush and brushing my hair very hard. "There," she said at last. "You look like you belong to someone now." I stared at myself in the mirror. I looked like Lord Snooty out of the Beano.

The school I had to go to was miles up the hill. My Grandma came with me. She knocked on a small window and a big woman told us to come in and wait in a room. While we were waiting, Grandma sorted my hair out again, and straightened my tie. Then she kissed me goodbye. "Now be a good lad and work hard. See you later on." She fetched a big red apple out of her pocket and said, "Here, eat this at play time, and don't go giving it away."

I waited for about ten minutes on my own. A small grey haired man in a hairy jacket came into the room. He looked at me, then he looked at a piece of paper on the top of a desk. He said: "Richards?"

I said: "Yes."

He looked at me very hard. "We don't have new boys in this school very often. Where were you before you came here?"

"Germany."

"Dad in the army, eh?"

I didn't say anything. Something made him look at his piece of paper again.

"Oh. You live with your Grandma, oh I see, well er, let's get you along to Mr Harmer.*

Mrs Mustow! Mrs Mustow!"

A door opened and a big lady came in. "Take, er, Richards here to Mr Harmer's class will you Mrs Mustow?"

There were tiles on the walls of the corridors and noises echoed from a distance. A boy came towards us with a dog. As he passed he said, "It just keeps following me into school, Mrs Mustow. There's nothing I can do."

"I bet you whistle it all the way here, just so's you can take it home. We're not daft Booth. We all know you by now." *

As he passed by, the boy stuck his tongue out at me, for no reason at all as far as I could tell. "If you're anything like that one, you'd better go home now," Mrs Mustow said. "One of Mr Booth in a school this size, is quite enough."

*Stop to discuss inference.

UNIT 10 School Days — Highlight English — 55

My new grey shirt itched like mad and my shoes squeaked and were rubbing my heels. We stopped at the last door of the corridor and Mrs Mustow knocked and someone shouted, "Come!" As we went in all the kids started to stand up, but when they saw it was us, they sat down. Mrs Mustow handed the teacher a big envelope then turned to me. "Have you got your dinner money?" I took the apple out of my pocket and then I fished out an envelope and handed it to her. She took it and went out.

I was standing by the teacher's desk. Every kid in the class was looking at me. I knew I was bright red. I put the apple back in my pocket and it made a big bulge. I felt stupid. I thought I was going to explode with heat and I was sure I could feel blood running down my back from where my shirt had cut a big hole in my neck.

The teacher took no notice of me and just carried on with me standing by the desk. "Now Class Four, I'm going to ask you one more time and if I don't get a sensible answer there's going to be no games this afternoon. For the last time, where do kippers come from?" ‡

The class was silent. No one moved. One by one the kids looked down as Mr Harmer looked at them. "No one. Not one of you. I bet you all eat them though, don't you? Have you never thought where they come from? Learning isn't just what we teach you, it's learning to think for yourself, to ask questions. So, you're having kipper for breakfast and you think: "This isn't like the fish I get at the fish and chip shops or like the fish I have at school on Fridays, so you ask someone and find out and that's where your general knowledge comes from. Isn't it Shirley?" A girl nodded dumbly. "So that's it then. No games for you this afternoon."

I knew about kippers. Uncle Douglas told me. He knew, because he sold fish on the market. A boy had his hand up. "Sir, that's not fair Sir, because Booth isn't here Sir. He might know." Mr Harmer moaned a long moan.

"We'll see then. In Booth's mighty brain lies the fate of the Class Four games lesson. We shall ask him, if, and I repeat if, he returns." ‡

He looked at me for the first time. "Where shall we put you? We're a bit short of room at the moment. Would you mind sitting next to Penelope, until we have a think what to do with you?" The class laughed and whistled. I was red enough to blow up. All the kids were grinning and pulling faces and Mr Harmer was saying: "All right. That will do, that will do."

The space was right at the back of the room. Penelope turned away from me and squashed herself to the other end of the bench. Mr Harmer said: "I'm sure Penelope will look after you, won't you Penelope?"

She was as red as me. She had a white fluffy cardigan and long brown wavy hair. I sat and stared down at my desk top. My eyes were full of tears, and I breathed deeply to stop myself crying. At last a boy came round with some paper and pens and I could start writing, and once I got on with that it was almost the same as being at my old school.

After about half an hour the door opened and the boy Booth came in.
"Aha. Mr Booth returns." ‡

"Sorry I was so long Sir. My mother wasn't in so I had to go round to my Aunty's to get the key, but she wasn't in either and..."

"Thank you Booth. That will do. As long as the beast is well clear of the premises, I don't mind what you've done with it."

Booth started to walk to his seat, which was immediately in front of Mr Harmer's desk; but Mr Harmer called him back. "Don't go to your seat just yet, for we have a little question for you. Now listen carefully, Booth. If you get the answer wrong, we shall be doing sums all

‡ *Stop for anticipation activity – what will happen next?*
  – why do you think this?

afternoon. If, by any strange chance, you should get it right, you shall be out playing games with Mr Turner, while I recover from shock in the staffroom."

"Now Booth. Here's the question. Where do kippers come from? While you were out, the combined intelligence of Class Four discovered that neither "The Fish Shop" or "Out of the Sea' were a satisfactory answer. So, Booth, what do you think?"

The class was absolutely silent as Booth tried to think. He screwed up his forehead and looked round the room for ideas. "Well, Booth?"

"Hang on, Sir."

"Well get a move on, lad."

Penelope said under her breath, "He'll never get it. He's the biggest dope in the class." Without meaning to, I whispered to her,

"I know the answer."

"That's it. Time up, Booth. What's the answer? Do you know it?

"From Scarborough, Sir."

"No, Booth. Not from Scarborough." There was a huge moan from the class. "No good moaning. No one knows the answer. Too much football and netball and turning cartwheels at every verse end, and not enough reading and proper learning. No one knows the answer, so we'll stay in and do some proper work."

Penelope's hand was up. ‡ "Please, Sir. He knows the answer, and he's in our class, Sir."

The room fell silent again. Mr Harmer pointed to the front of the room where Booth had been standing. I walked forward, going red again, and again, feeling the tears burning the back of my eyes. I wanted to go home. To be away from this horrible room with tiles half way up the walls, where everyone of the kids stared at me without speaking. Mr Harmer looked at me. "Go on then. Where do kippers come from?"

It flashed in my mind that Uncle Douglas was always telling stories and making things up. I wasn't sure what to say. "Well?"

"Well, my uncle says they start off as herrings and then they're smoked over the fire in sheds, and that's where they come from."

"Why did your uncle tell you that?"

"Because I asked him, Sir."

"You see. Just what I was saying. General knowledge comes from asking questions. Did you ever ask your uncle where kippers came from Booth?"

"No, Sir."

"No, I bet you didn't. Well, there we are, so you can all go to games after all, thanks to Richards here. I can tell you lot though, it makes me ashamed to think that none of you knew the answer, and that you had to rely on a new boy to help you out."

I walked back to my seat. None of the kids seemed pleased that I had got the answer right. * Outside, a bell rang. As I sat down, my chin started to wobble like it did before I cried. The room emptied. Mr Harmer came down to my desk. "It's play time. Go out and have a run round and eat that apple."

Outside, the playground was full of kids all running about and shouting. I didn't know anybody, so I stood by the door. I didn't know whether to eat the apple or not. It was so big and red, I thought everyone would look at me if I started to eat it. So I kept it in my pocket and decided to eat it at dinner time.

‡ After a minute or so, Booth and some other boys from the class came over. "We've been looking for you. ‡ You've got us into trouble." I stared at them. They looked very big and their clothes were not new like mine. "I saved you from missing football..." I began.

‡ *Stop for anticipation activity – what will happen next?*
– why do you think this?

* *Stop to discuss inference.*

UNIT 10 School Days — Highlight English — 57

"Don't be daft. He's always like that on Mondays, going on about not letting us do games. But he always does in the end."

I didn't know what to say. They were stood round me in a ring, pressing in, close. I couldn't swallow. I could hardly breathe. There seemed to be kids all round me. "So. We're going to fight you."

I told them I didn't want to fight, but they said that I had to. My blazer was pulled off from behind and laid down on the playground, and several kids stood on it. Booth grabbed my neck. Then he let it go, and dashed off. The other kids followed him. A teacher came over and asked if I was all right and I said I was. My blazer was all messy though. And the apple in the pocket, the big red apple that Grandma had polished on her apron and given me, had been squashed, flat.

Back in the class, Mr Harmer asked me what had happened. I told him that I'd fallen over. ‡ "Not over Booth's foot, I hope. He does have a habit of leaving them lying about in the playground." I said it wasn't over Booth's foot and Mr Harmer said I could go and sit down.

On my desk was a piece of paper folded over. On the front it said, "To the New Boy." Round that, someone had drawn wavy lines in different colours. Inside it said: "I'm glad you knew the answer, from..." Then there were question marks in red and blue and yellow.

I looked around but no-one was looking at me now, and I started to do some more writing, and I hoped that the note was from Penelope, with the fluffy cardigan and long, wavy hair.

By Hamish Whiteley

‡ *Stop for anticipation activity – what will happen next?*
– why do you think this?

PUNCTUATION

Full stops
One of the problems with full stops is that pupils cannot always judge when a sentence is complete. For those children who can do this verbally as in Activity 1, page 44 of the Pupil's Book but have difficulty using full stops correctly in their own writing, there are a number of ways of helping with punctuation, not already covered.
1 Pupils who read fairly fluently and convey the meaning with good pausing and intonation can be helped to punctuate their own written work by the following procedure:
a The pupils read what they have written aloud making a small pencil mark at the point where they pause.
b When all the marks have been made, they then go back to the first place they paused and hold their pencil at the first mark they made.
c They then read up to the point where they made the mark and ask themselves the question: "Is that a sentence?" If the answer is "Yes", then they put in the full stop. If the answer is "No" they move their pencil to the next mark along. They then read the whole piece again and ask the question: "Is that a sentence?" Once they have found the first sentence, they then go on to the next point and work from there.

This sounds more involved than it is. Many pupils find this a very helpful method and quickly substitute reading aloud for reading silently.
2 For pupils who just need their memory about full stops jogging occasionally there are two short activities that are amusing and quite effective.
a Pupils sit in a small group with the teacher present. The idea is that they take it in turns to tell each other news of some kind, e.g. what they did at the weekend, but every time they reach the end of a sentence they have to add the word "Full Stop" e.g. "I helped Dad on the allotment. (FULL STOP) Then we went to see Nan. (FULL STOP)" This activity could also be done between the teacher and pupil, for about thirty seconds when a pupil comes to have a book marked.
b In a similar group each person takes it in turn to contribute one word of a story or piece of information. The person finishing a sentence says the last word and then "Full Stop". This is a very useful activity for all kinds of other reasons including the need to listen carefully and retain the story.

Comma
Pupils using the first suggestion to help with full stops can use the same method to help with commas; that is, when they have paused and a full stop is not required, very often it is the appropriate place for a comma.

Speech marks
Very often one of the main problems with speech marks is establishing what goes in the speech marks. For pupils with this problem, using comics with speech bubbles can be helpful. Rather like the work sheets in this series, pupils can use a comic of their choice and practise writing sentences about what is happening, putting the words in the speech bubbles into speech marks.

Pupils may need the word "indent" explaining prior to working on the work sheets for paragraphs and speech marks.

PUNCTUATION (SENTENCES)

ACTIVITY 1: on your own

Put the words in the sentences below in the right order.
Write down each sentence.
Remember: Put a capital letter at the beginning and a full stop at the end.

1 full bus the is _____

2 my that is rubber _____

3 left no there milk is _____

4 coffee never Mum my drinks _____

5 must home be you tea for _____

6 sweets are those my _____

ACTIVITY 2: on your own

Use the picture on the right to answer the questions below.
Write down the answers in complete sentences.

1 How many people are waiting for the bus?
2 Why do you think the baby is crying?
3 What is going to happen to the woman's shopping?
4 How do you know that the girls are sisters?
5 What time of the year do you think it is?

1 _____
2 _____
3 _____
4 _____
5 _____

ACTIVITY 3: on your own

Write four sentences to describe the picture on the left.

1 _____
2 _____
3 _____
4 _____

PUNCTUATION (QUESTION MARKS)

ACTIVITY 1: on your own

Write a question for each of the pictures below.
Start the question with the word under the picture.
Remember: Begin with a capital letter and end with a question mark.

who   how   which

why   where   when

1 _____
2 _____
3 _____
4 _____
5 _____
6 _____

ACTIVITY 2: on your own

Look at the picture below.
Write down five questions the boy might ask the alien.
Start the questions with one of the words under the pictures above.

Punctuation ——————— *Highlight English* ——————— 61

PUNCTUATION (CAPITAL LETTERS)

ACTIVITY 1: on your own

Where there is a star, make up a name and write it in.
Remember: Begin with a capital letter.

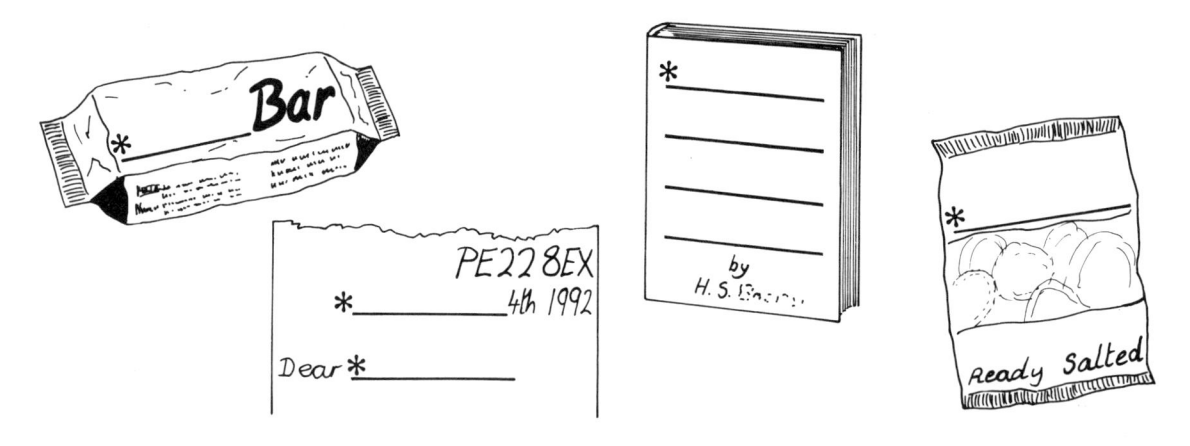

ACTIVITY 2: on your own

Fill in the blanks with the word asked for.
Remember: Each word will begin with a capital letter.

It all happened when we were on our way to school. We were just crossing _____ (name of road) Road, when a car came screaming round the corner. The car was a _____ (name of car) and there were two men in it. The car was going very fast and could not get round the corner. It crashed into the shop window of _____ (name of shop). There was an awful mess. There were cans of _____ (name of a drink) and packets of _____ (name of sweets) all over the road. The car did not stop. It shot off up Kington Road. I expect it's in _____ (name of town) by now.

Mr _____ (surname), who works in the shop, said he knew it was going to be a bad day because it was _____ (name of day) the 13th.

PUNCTUATION (Speech marks)

ACTIVITY 1: on your own

Write 6 sentences for each of the speech bubbles below.
For the last three, make up your own words to go in the speech bubbles.

Points to remember:

1. start speech marks
2. Capital letter
3. Punctuation mark
4. Close speech marks
5. Full stop

"I'm going to join the PE club," Elin said.

Andi — "Have you seen Mum?"

Mrs. Singh — "Two pounds please"

Mr. Short — "She's gone into town"

Kellie

Lee

Alsha

1 _____
2 _____
3 _____
4 _____
5 _____
6 _____

PUNCTUATION (SPEECH MARKS)

You can make a sentence more interesting by telling the reader more about what is happening:
1 "I don't feel very well," moaned Rafiq, <u>putting his head on the desk.</u>

ACTIVITY 1: on your own

Using the idea in 1 above, write interesting sentences for 1 – 6 below. Work out your own words for the speech bubbles.
Point to remember: Add a comma before the extra details.

1 Helen
2 Mr Brennan
3 Jayne
4 Kylie
5 Steve
6 Ceri

1 _____
2 _____
3 _____
4 _____
5 _____
6 _____

PUNCTUATION (PARAGRAPHS)

ACTIVITY 1: on your own

The boxes 1 and 2 below show what happens when Tom gets up late. You are going to write 2 paragraphs to describe what happens. Each box gives enough details for one paragraph.
Starting with Box 1, write a sentence to describe what is happening in A, eg: Tom woke up with a shock. Then write a sentence about what is happening in B, C and D.

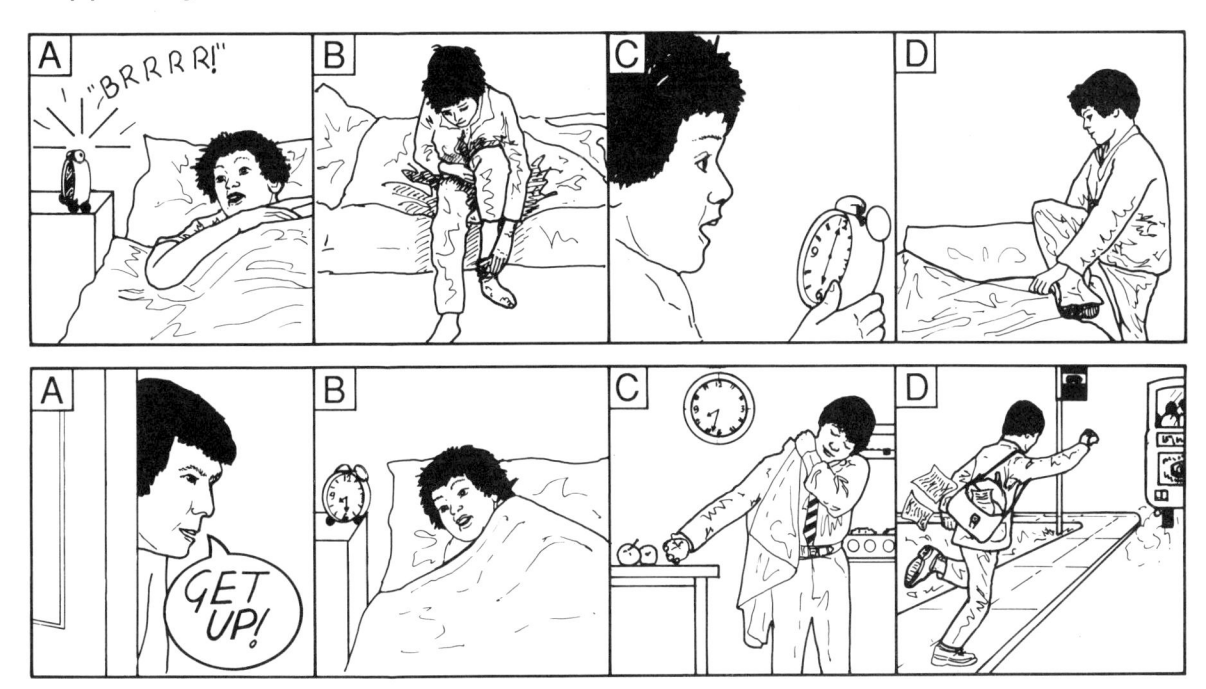

Start a new paragraph for Box 2 and in the same way, write four sentences.
Remember: Indent the first sentences of each paragraph.

SPELLING

Introduction and Overview
This advice aims to help children of secondary school age who have received primary education but who still have some problems.

The spelling pages in the Teacher's Pack have been written so that they can be used as homework sheets.

Words of a phonically regular pattern

1 **How to establish where a pupil should start on spelling help.**
The first thing to do is to establish at what point to start spelling help. One way to do this is to find the pupil's BASE LINE, that is, the earliest point at which spelling is falling down.

2 **How to do this.**
There is a fairly well established progression for teaching spellings.

LEVEL:

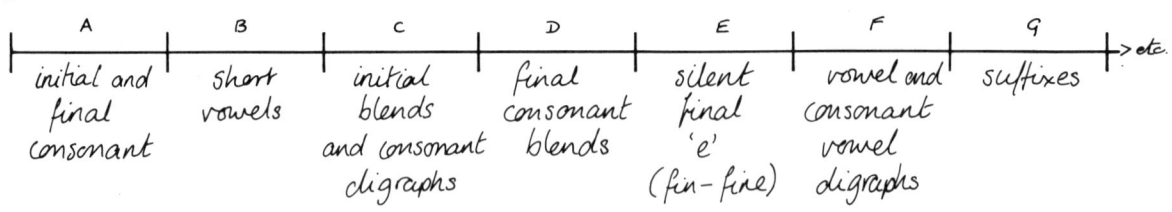

A	B	C	D	E	F	G
initial and final consonant	short vowels	initial blends and consonant digraphs	final consonant blends	silent final 'e' (fin-fine)	vowel and consonant vowel digraphs	suffixes

→ etc.

Find a piece of the pupil's FREE writing, that is unaided writing that has not been copied. Using the line above, which is only a brief indication of the phonic progression, look at your pupil's spelling errors and see how far to the left of this line errors fall. e.g.

Owr dog is baed he braks

(Our dog is bad he barks)

Owr – a difficult word; may be better taught on its own (see 7 below).
baed – short vowel possibly weak, though "dog" was spelt correctly (Level B).
Braks – some letters in the wrong order; may not know "ar" sound (Level F).

As can be seen, the base line for the pupil above is at the short vowel level. This then, might be where to start, but it is worth checking on previous pieces of free writing to make sure that this was not a one-off spelling error at this level. If it has happened a few other times, you can be fairly sure that it is right to start at the short vowel level.

Once you have established where to start, it is usually a sound principle to continue through the progression in the order above, (given that spelling problems are occurring at the various points). One exception to this, is where a pupil has fairly good spelling and is just falling down here and there on one or two points.

Tips once base line established

3 **Helping pupils remember sounds.**
Make a card for each phonic rule. Put the letter or letter combination on one side (Fig 1(i)). Discuss with the pupil the word that would help him to remember the sound, then he can draw it on the other side (Fig 1(ii)). The pupil is far more likely to remember the sound if he has chosen his own word for it.

A pocket can be taped on to the back of an exercise book so that an envelope containing the cards can be kept securely in the back (Fig 1(iii)).

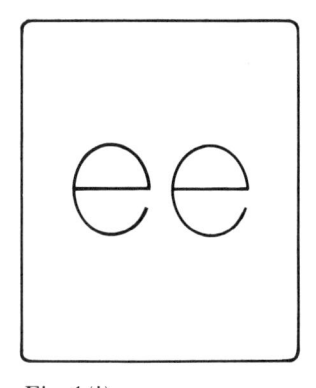

Fig 1(i) 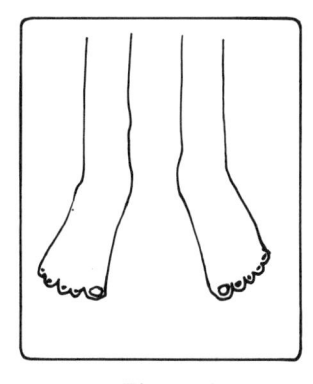　　　　　　　　　Fig 1 (ii) 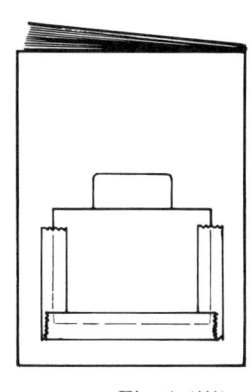　　　　　　　　　Fig 1 (iii)

4 Helping pupils remember patterns and which words have the same pattern.

Pupils can be helped to remember the pattern in words by writing a list of words that exemplify a rule. A coloured pencil or highlighter can be used to highlight the rule within each word, e.g. the vowel digraph "ee" (See Fig 2(i)).

Also, the pupil can draw a small picture in his exercise book to help remember the sound and write a sentence trying to use as many of the words as possible (Fig 2 (i)). Reference and further details: Gill Cotterell.

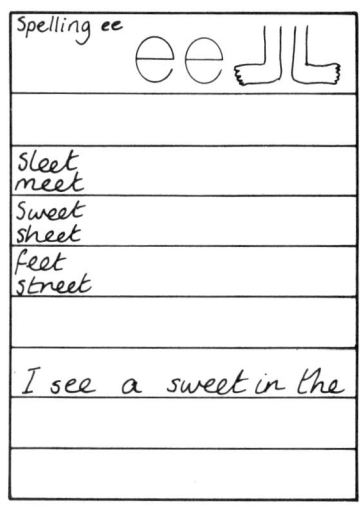

Fig 2(i) 　　　　　　　　　Fig 2 (ii)

5 Helping pupils with polysyllabic words.

In a word like "remember", a common error is to miss out a syllable, e.g. "rember". This problem can be helped by encouraging the pupil to hear the syllables in a word. Practice can be given by asking the pupil/pupils how many syllables there are, for example in the word "garden". The pupil then claps out each syllable, saying the syllable at the same time. Once the procedure is established, children can be encouraged to get into the habit of tapping out the syllables in words that they want to spell using the tip of their pen.

To this activity can be added the rule that every syllable must have a vowel.

6 Using the mouth to help with spelling.

Many children with spelling problems have no idea what is happening in their mouth. They may not realise for example, that they put their lips together to form "m" or use their tongue to form "n".

For some children it is very helpful to ask them to tell you, for example, what their tongue is doing when they say the letter "n".

This type of activity can help the pupil to feel some initial and final consonants (e.g. "m" or "n"); initial and final blends (e.g. "pl" or "st"); and for letter order in general. Reference and further details: Edith Norrie.

Some of the activities focus on consonants in various positions in words and give the opportunity for practice in this kind of awareness, e.g. Pupil's Book page 53 (Act. 1 & 2); page 56 (Act. 1); page 58 (Act. 1). Teacher's Pack page 72 (Act. 2).

Beware of adding the "schwa" sound to letters. The schwa sound is made by adding a vowel sound, usually 'uh', after a consonant. For example the letter 'm' 'says' 'mmmmmmm' but with the schwa sound added says 'muh'. Schwa sounds are hard to avoid in letters like 'b', but must be avoided because they can confuse some children, e.g. 'duh' 'o' 'guh' spells 'duoger' not 'dog'.

Problem words

7 **Remembering problem words by using mnemonics.**

Some words do not follow a rule or present a regular pattern, e.g. "bough"; "island". Other words may follow a pattern but the pattern just does not help the child to remember the spelling, e.g. "said"; "our"; "because".

One way to help the pupil remember words such as these, is to encourage the pupils themselves to think of ways to remember. For example, a pupil who invariably spelt "said" incorrectly, suddenly spotted that the word "aid", which he could spell, was embedded in it. That was enough for him never to forget how to spell "said". Similarly another pupil remembered "island" as an "island is land". Once a pupil has thought of a way of remembering a word, he can use a page of his book to record it.

9 **Using kinaesthetic memory.**

Some children have a good memory for the "feel" of a word and can benefit by writing a word, with their finger, in joined writing on to a pre-prepared soft surface or just on to a desk or table. Alternatively the teacher can write the word to be learnt on a strip of paper n large clear cursive writing and the pupil can trace the letters with his finger (Fig 2(ii)). A parent could well help here, as only a few key words at a time should be learnt, practising each day for a week. Reference and further details: Lynette Bradley.

REFERENCES

Lynette Bradley	"Visual memory and phonological skills" in "Reading and Spelling Backwardness" by Lynette Bradley and Peter Bryant, published in *Psychological Research* 1981, 43: 193-199
Gill Cotterell	*Teaching the Non-reading dyslexic child*, LDA 1985
Edith Norrie	Edith Norrie Lettercase from the Helen Arkell Centre in London

SPELLING (SHORT VOWEL)

Links with pages 54 & 55 in Pupil's Book.

ACTIVITY 1: on your own

Write down the words for the pictures below.
All the words will end in 'ap'.

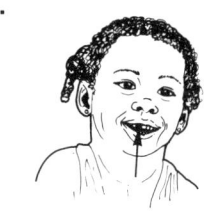

ACTIVITY 2: on your own

Make words by joining some of the letters on the left to "an".
Watch out, not all of the letters will make words.
Write down the words you make.
Write the words for the pictures.

Spelling — Highlight English — 69

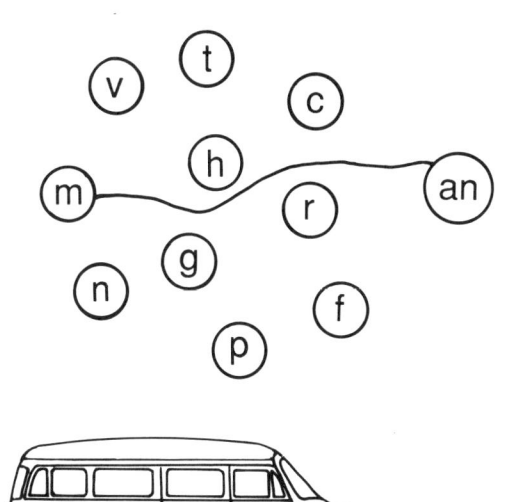

SPELLING (SHORT VOWEL)

Links with pages 54 & 55 in Pupil's Book.

ACTIVITY 1: on your own

Using the square below, write down the words you can make ending in 'ill'. Then write down the words for the pictures on the right.

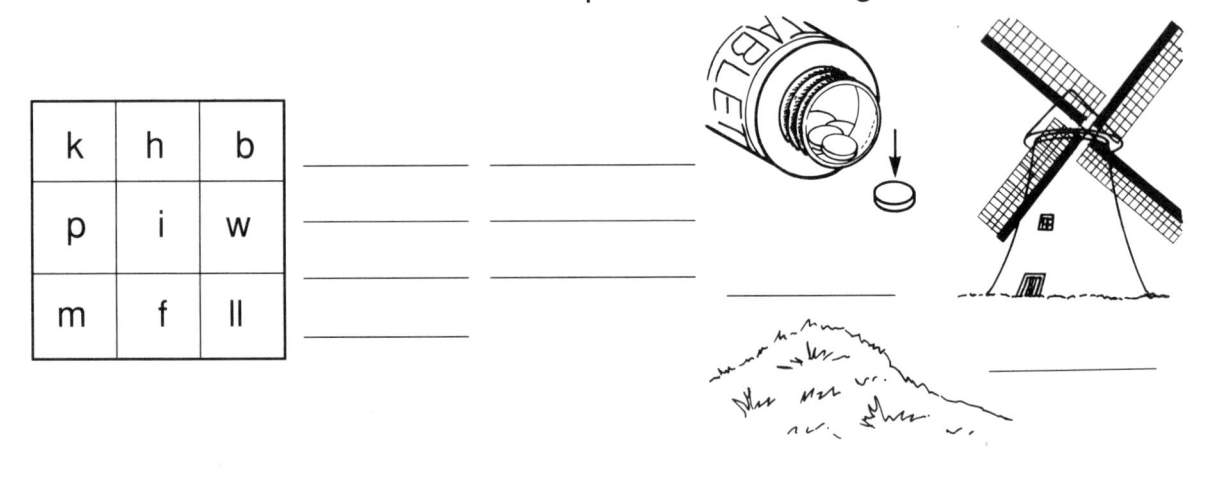

k	h	b
p	i	w
m	f	ll

ACTIVITY 2: on your own or with a partner

Use each of the letters in the first box below.
Match the letter with 'in' and 'ip' from the second box.
Write down the ones that make words.
Write down the words for the pictures on the right.

| b | d | r | f | t | p | n | l | s |

| in | ip |

bin   dip

SPELLING (INITIAL BLENDS)

Links with pages 56 & 57 in Pupil's Book.

ACTIVITY 1: on your own

Ring round words which begin with "sp" and "st". There are no diagonals.
Write down the words you find.
Picking words from your list, write the words for the pictures below.

s	t	i	f	f	s	q	s	z
u	s	n	l	s	t	a	b	o
s	t	i	c	k	u	p	o	h
e	o	s	t	a	c	k	n	k
s	p	i	l	l	k	e	m	s
x	f	p	s	g	e	s	p	t
p	y	s	p	i	n	b	j	i
o	u	d	o	s	p	e	l	l
s	p	i	t	o	s	p	u	l

spit

ACTIVITY 2: on your own

Write down the words you can make using the letter square below.
All the words must begin with 'gr'.

m	gr	ll
a	i	p
b	n	d

SPELLING (INITIAL BLENDS) Links with pages 56 & 57 in Pupil's Book.

ACTIVITY 1: on your own

Use the letters on 1 - 7 to make words beginning with 'tr' and 'sk'.
Write the words down in two lists.

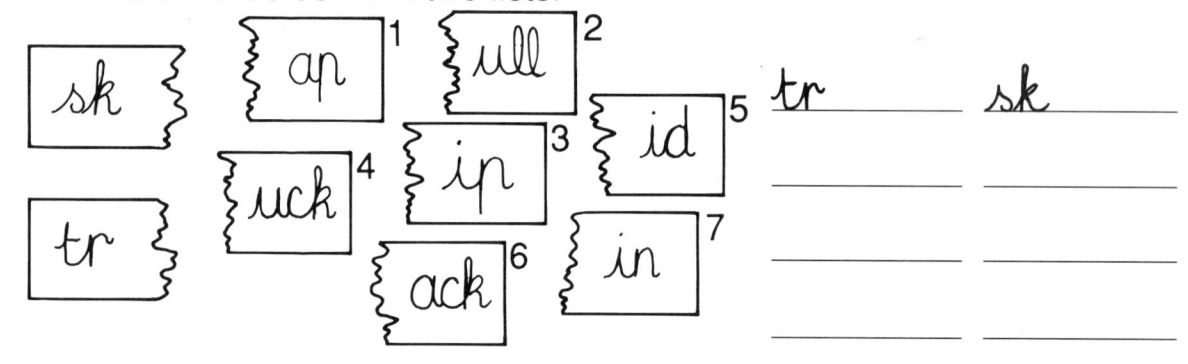

sk

tr

1. ap
2. ull
3. ip
4. uck
5. id
6. ack
7. in

tr _____   sk _____

ACTIVITY 2: on your own

Write the words for the pictures below.
Write out the words again, putting them into one of the lists.
List A is for words where the second letter in 'r'.
List B is for words where the second letter is 'l'.

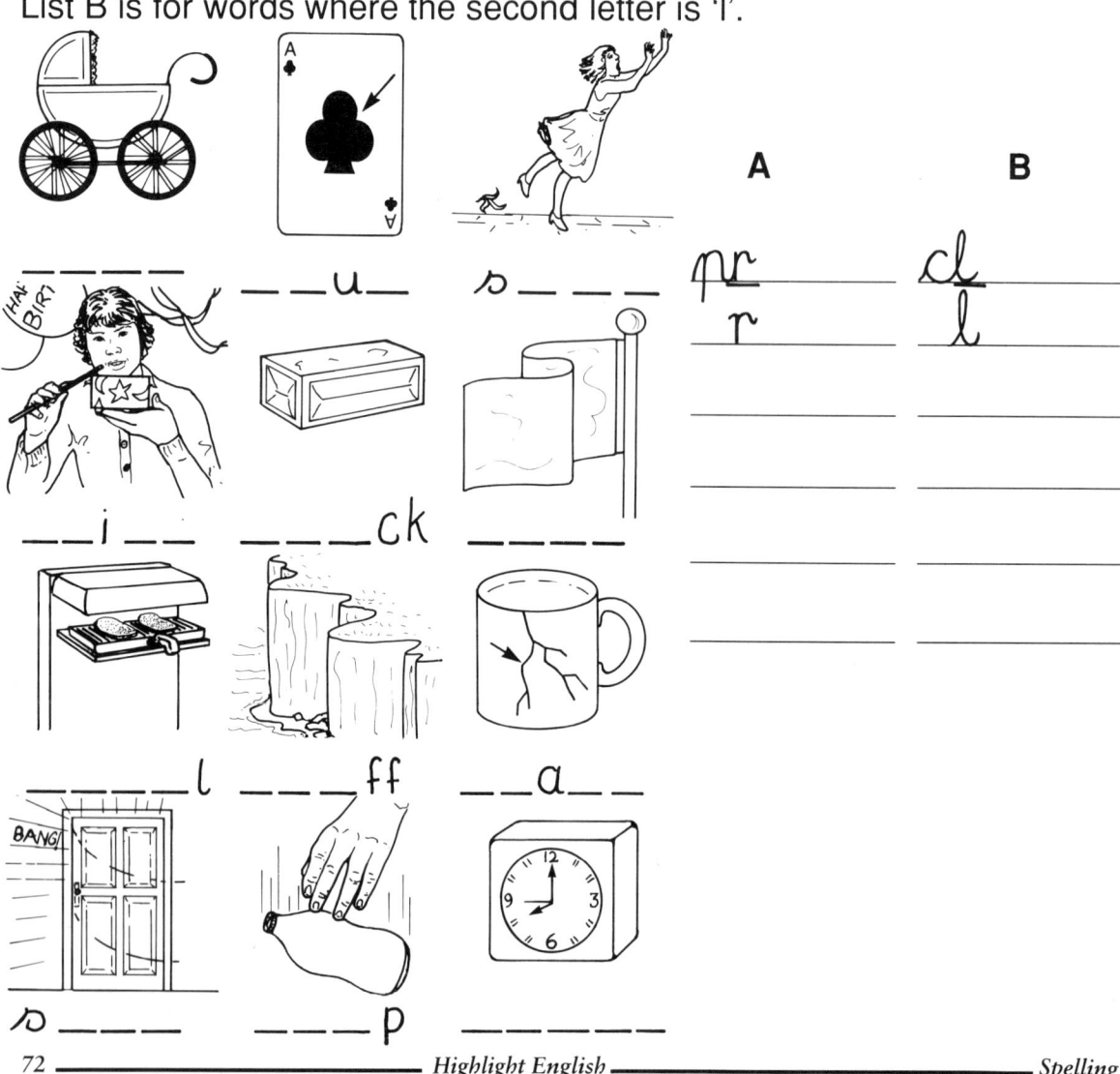

A   B

pr   cl
r   l

__u__   p____

__i__   ____ck   ____

__l__   ____ff   __a__

p____   ____p   ____

SPELLING (FINAL BLENDS) Links with page 58 in Pupil's Book.

ACTIVITY 1: on your own

Write down the missing words in the sentences below.
Each word will end with 'mp'.
Then fill in the word tree on the right.

ACROSS
2 If you hurt your leg, you will _ i _ _ .
4 A bit wet: d _ _ _ .
6 You feel poorly if you catch
  _ u _ _ s .
7 We went over a b _ _ _ in the road.

DOWN
1 A camel has a h _ _ _ .
2 Put another l _ _ _ of coal on the fire.
3 A pain you sometimes get:
  c r _ _ _ .
5 "That made you _ u _ _ ," Darren said with a grin.

ACTIVITY 2: on your own

Make words by joining the letters on the left with 'sk' or 'ft'.
Write down the words that you make.
Put four of the words into a sentence.

left

1 _____
2 _____
3 _____
4 _____

Spelling ——————— Highlight English ——————— 73

SPELLING (FINAL BLENDS)

Links with pages 58 in Pupil's Book.

ACTIVITY 1: on your own

Write down the missing words in the sentences below.
Each word will end in 'nd'.
Then fill in the word tree on the right.

ACROSS
2 There is a lot of _ _ _ _ at the seaside.
4 There's a sharp _ e _ _ at the bottom of the hill.
5 Cats always seem to l _ _ _ on their feet.
6 "That's the _ _ _ ," Mr Jepsom said. "Time for bed."
7 "I can't st _ _ _ that man," Gareth muttered.

DOWN
1 To put something together again: m _ _ _ _ .
2 I am going to s _ _ _ her a birthday card.
3 The fish _ _ _ chip shop is in Oxford Road.
4 Have you got a rubber b _ _ _ ?
5 "I'm not going to _ e _ _ him 50p again."

ACTIVITY 2: on your own

Write down the words you can make using the 'ind' and 'old' pattern.
Using words from your list, write down the words for 1 - 4 below.

bl, f, k, m, w, r → ind

c, g, s, f, h, t → old

blind   *cold*

74 — Highlight English — Spelling

SPELLING (FINAL BLENDS)

Links with page 58 in Pupil's Book.

ACTIVITY 1: on your own

Ring round the words with 'all' in them.
There are no diagonal words.
Write down the words you find.
Then write down the words for the pictures below.

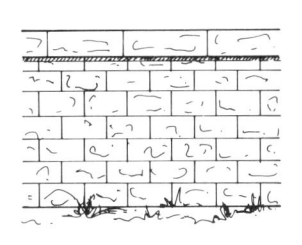

y	l	a	r	a	l	l	i
u	z	s	y	w	a	l	l
h	o	m	u	s	z	b	k
s	b	a	f	t	l	a	c
t	a	l	l	a	f	e	a
o	v	l	d	l	a	h	l
l	e	b	a	l	l	c	l
d	a	l	l	q	l	d	u

small _____   _____

_____   _____

_____   _____

_____

_____   _____   _____   _____

ACTIVITY 2: on your own

Longer words that begin with the sound 'all', usually have only one 'l'.
Read the words in the box.
Fill the blanks in the sentences below, with one of the words from the box.

> always   almost   also   altogether

1 "I've _____ finished," Mark yelled.

2 We _____ go camping in the summer.

3 "Take out your Maths books," Mrs Bakshi said. "You will _____ need, a ruler, a compass and a pencil."

4 "You have made seventy pounds_____," Mr Willis said proudly.

SPELLING (TRIPLE BLENDS)

Follows on from page 58 in Pupil's Book.

ACTIVITY 1: on your own

Write down the words you can make beginning with "str".
Fill each gap in the sentences 1-4 with a word beginning with "str".

str — ip, etch, uck, ing, ong

1 The tree was _____ by lightning.
2 "I'm _____ , Miss," Amanda said. "I'll carry that."
3 "If you _____ that rubber band any more, it will snap," Anjali warned.
4 "I can't get this _____ of wallpaper off," moaned Becky.

ACTIVITY 2: on your own

Write down the missing word in the sentences below.
Each word will begin with 'scr'.
Fill in the word tree on the right.
Using the words from the word tree, write down the words for the pictures below.

ACROSS
1 That floor needs a good _ _ _ _ _ _ .
2 Pick up that _ _ _ a _ of paper.
3 Another way of saying, 'Go away!'
4 "You look a real _ _ _ _ _ _ _ . Brush your hair."

DOWN
1 Marcel hurt his knee in the _ _ _ u _ .
2 "That cat might _ _ _ _ t _ _ you," Mrs Chudy warned.

76 — Highlight English — Spelling

SPELLING (PLURALS) Links with page 59 in Pupil's Book.

ACTIVITY 1: on your own

To make most nouns plural, add an 's'.
Write down the words for the pictures below.

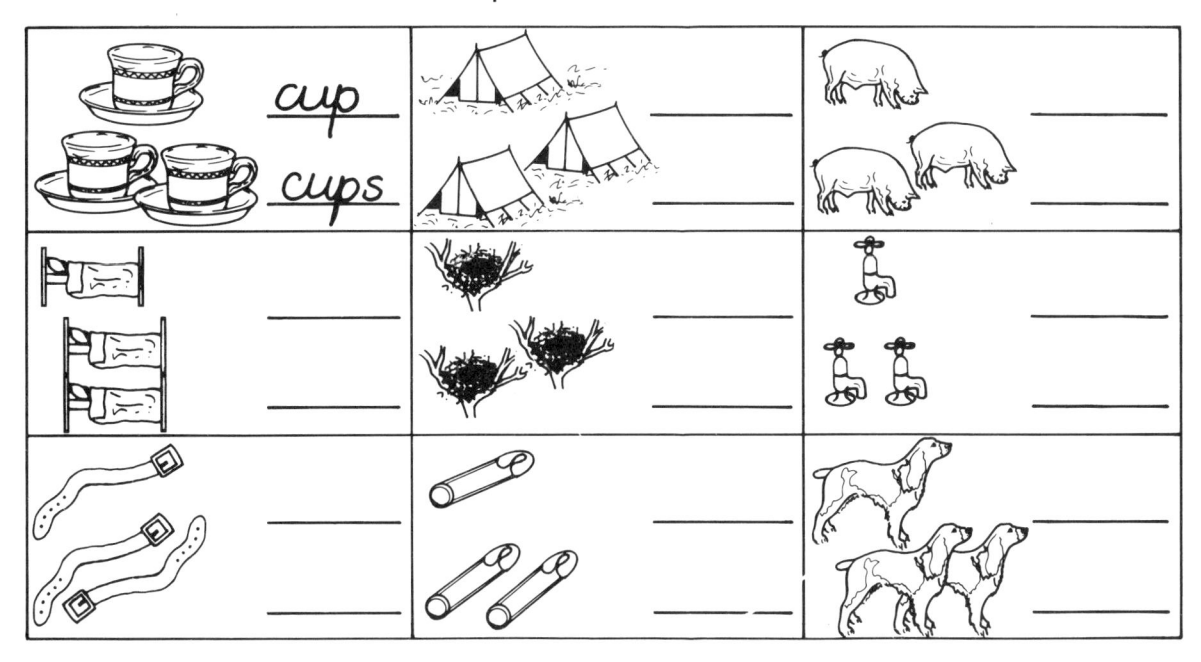

cup		
cups		

ACTIVITY 2: on your own or with a partner

To make words ending in 'x', 's', 'sh' and 'ch' plural, add 'es'.
Ring round the words ending in 'x', 's', 'sh' and 'ch'. There are no diagonals.
Write them down and then write their plurals next to them, as shown.
Then write down the words for the pictures below.

a	f	s	i	x	l	a	p
d	r	i	n	g	a	l	i
i	o	p	u	n	c	h	e
t	g	r	c	a	r	b	c
c	l	a	s	s	u	u	r
h	u	m	p	e	t	s	o
a	i	r	m	e	c	h	s
t	h	r	u	s	h	l	s

brush brushes

Spelling ———————— Highlight English ———————— 77

SPELLING (FINAL "E") Links with pages 60 & 61 in Pupil's Book.

ACTIVITY 1: on your own

Add the 'e' to the words in column B.
Use the words from columns **A** and **B** and write down the words for the pictures.
Then, write down the missing words in the sentences.

A	**B** e
hop	hop
rod	rod
slop	slop
pop	pop

1 He _____ his bike to school.
2 "I _____ you have laid the table," Mrs Burkitt said.
3 "You can borrow my fishing _____ ," Lizzie shouted.

ACTIVITY 2: on your own

Make words by joining the letters on the left with 'oke' and 'ole'.
Write down the words that you can make.
Write four sentences using as many of the words as you can.

joke   vole

1 _____
2 _____
3 _____
4 _____

SPELLING (FINAL "E") Links with pages 60 & 61 in Pupil's Book.

ACTIVITY 1: on your own

Add the 'e' to the words in column B.
Write down the words for the pictures.
The words will be in one of the columns.

A	B e
cut	cut
tub	tub
cub	cub

_____ _____ _____ _____ _____

ACTIVITY 2: on your own

Write down the missing words in the sentences below.
Fill in the word tree with words that end in 'e'.

DOWN
1 A month of the year: J _ _ _ .
2 A boy's name: L _ k _ .

ACROSS
3 "Play a t _ _ _ on the organ," Grandad said.
4 You need this to draw a straight line: _ _ l _ r .

ACTIVITY 3: on your own

Write down the missing words in the sentences below.
Fill in the word tree with words that end in 'use'.

DOWN
2 "E _ c _ _ _ me," the man said.
   "Is this the way to Chester?"

ACROSS
1 "You can _ _ _ my pen," Hedi whispered.
3 If the lights go out with a bang, you
   may need a new f _ _ _ .
4 "Can you _ m _ _ _ yourselves for
   a minute?" Mr Lund asked.

Spelling —————— *Highlight English* —————— 79

SPELLING (PAST TENSE)

Links with pages 62 & 63 in Pupil's Book.

Present tense tells you that something is happening now.
Past tense tells you that something happened in the past e.g. yesterday.
  Rule: To turn most verbs into the past tense, add 'ed'.
Present tense: I need two pounds.
Past tense: I needed two pounds.

ACTIVITY 1: on your own

Fill the blank in the sentences below with the word in the first bracket.
Put the word in the tense asked for: second bracket.

1 I _____ a cup of tea. (want) (present tense)
2 Darren _____ it was time to go home. (wish) (past tense)
3 We _____ football every Sunday. (play) (present tense)
4 The school _____ to buy a mini-bus. (want) (past tense)
5 I _____ the box up carefully. (lift) (past tense)
6 "Help me to _____ these up," Jola said. (pick) (present tense)

ACTIVITY 2: on your own

Fill the blanks in the sentences below with the word in brackets.
Put all the words into the past tense.
Remember: When a word has **one** vowel and ends in **one** consonant,
                double the final consonant before adding 'ed',
                except words ending in 'w', 'x' or 'y'.

e.g. hop   hopped
                  — double the consonant
one vowel   one end consonant

1 Mr Simpson _____ everywhere for the letter. (hunt)
2 We _____ talking when Mrs Evans came in. (stop)
3 The paper dart _____ on Mr Robson's desk. (land)
4 We _____ at a hotel, when we went on holiday. (stay)
5 Carly _____ her Dad to let her go to the disco. (beg)
6 The boy's hair _____ awful. (look)
7 The dog _____ the stick and _____ her tail. (drop, wag)

SPELLING (VOWEL DIGRAPH "EE")

ACTIVITY 1: on your own

Make words by joining the letters on the left with 'eet' and 'eep'.
Write down the words that you make.
Write down the words for the pictures below.

sleet

ACTIVITY 2: on your own

Write down the words for the pictures below.
All of the words end in 'eed'.

1 _____ 2 _____ 3 _____ 4 _____ 5 _____

SPELLING (VOWEL DIGRAPH "EE")

ACTIVITY 1: on your own

Write down the words that can be made using the 'eer' pattern below. Write down the words for the pictures on the right.

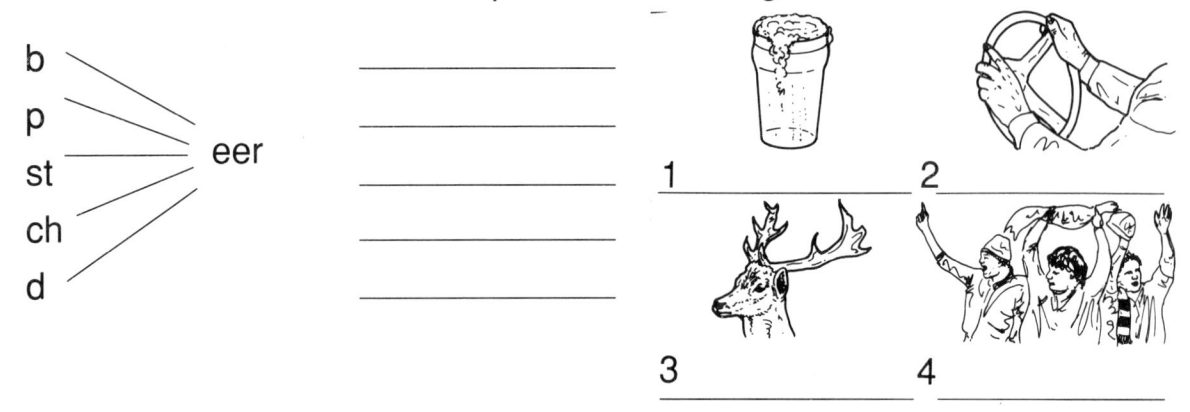

b
p
st   eer
ch
d

1 _____ 2 _____
3 _____ 4 _____

ACTIVITY 2: on your own

Fill in each gap with a word that has the 'ee' pattern in the middle.

a "Where have you _____?" Jan said crossly. "I've waited twenty minutes."

b "Have you _____ my socks? I can't find them anywhere."

c "I don't _____ very well," Rakhi moaned.

d "You _____ a haircut," Dad said.

e "I will _____ you outside school, at four o'clock," she whispered.

ACTIVITY 3: on your own

Write one sentence, using all four words below.

sneeze   _____
freeze   _____
breeze   _____
wheeze   _____

ACTIVITY 4: on your own

Write down the words for the pictures below.

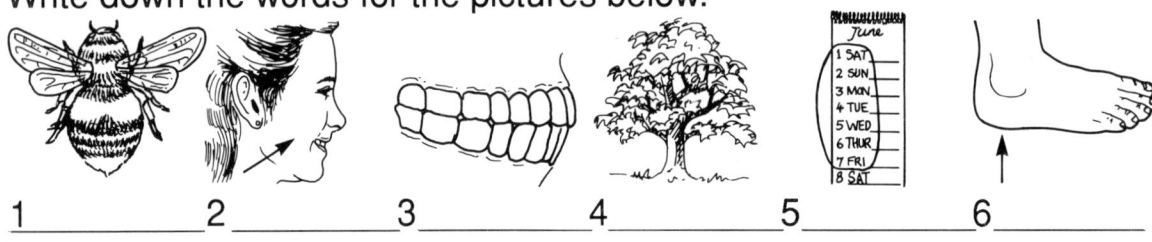

1 _____ 2 _____ 3 _____ 4 _____ 5 _____ 6 _____

CLASS:-

NAME	SPEAKING AND LISTENING TARGET 1															READING TARGET 2														
	LEVEL 2					LEVEL 3				LEVEL 4			LEVEL 5					LEVEL 2						LEVEL 3						LEVEL 4			LEVEL 5				
	a	b	c	d	e	a	b	c	d	a	b	c	d	a	b	c	d	e	a	b	c	d	e	f	a	b	c	d	e	f	a	b	c	d	a	b	c	d	e

Highlight English — 83

CLASS:-

NAME	WRITING														SPELLING 4										HANDWRITING				PRESENTATION		
	LEVEL 2				LEVEL 3					TARGET 3											LEVEL 2				LEVEL 3					4	L. 2		3	4	LEVEL 5		
										LEVEL 4					LEVEL 5																			
	a	b	c	d	a	b	c	d	e	a	b	c	d	e	a	b	c	d	e	a	b	c	d	a	b	c	d	a	a	a	b	c

84 ——— Highlight English ———

PRESENTATION 4/5

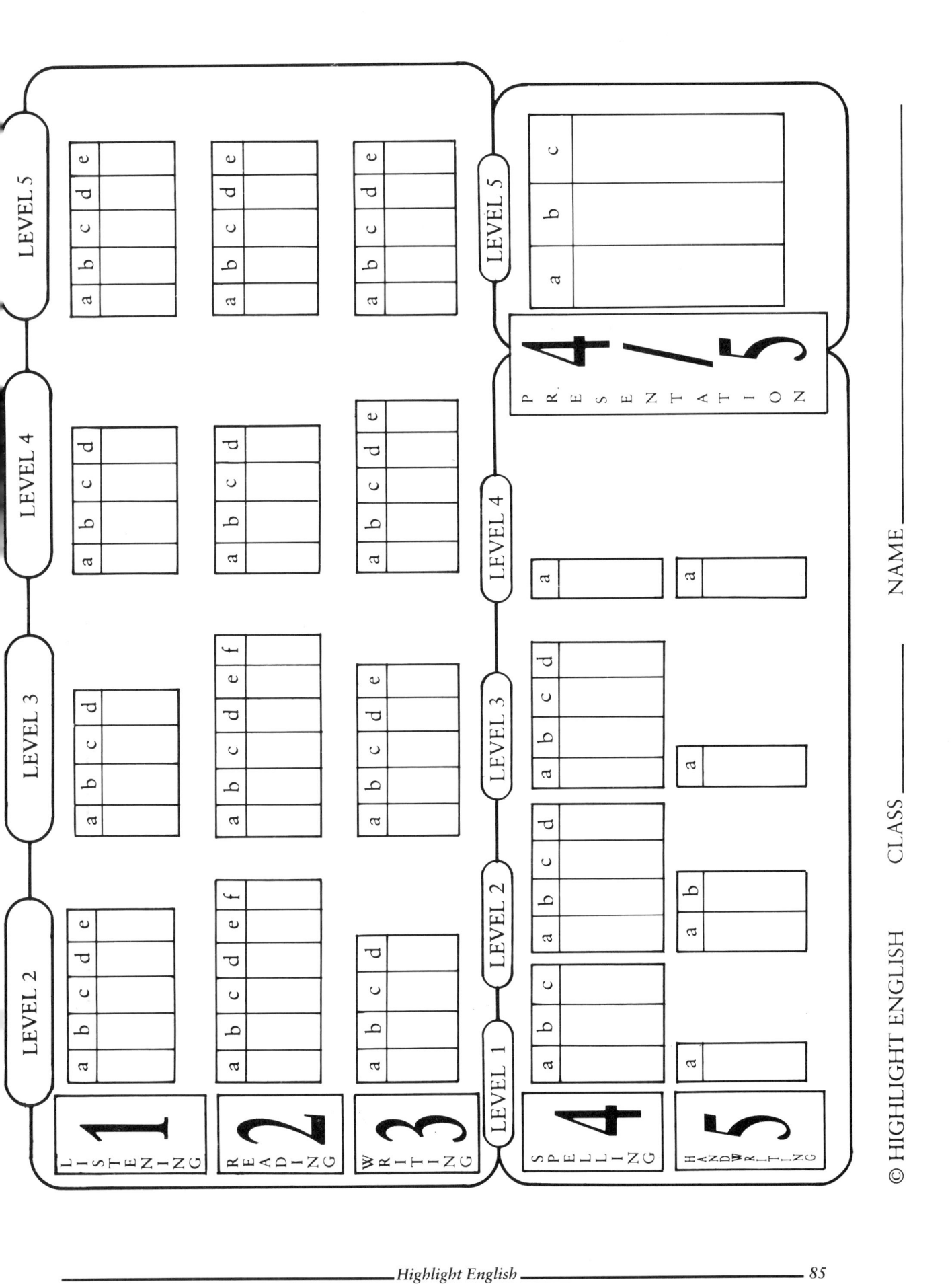

LEVEL 1

4 SPELLING

a	b	c	d

a	b	c	d

5 HANDWRITING

a

LEVEL 2

a	b	c	d

a	b

LEVEL 3

a	b	c	d

a

LEVEL 4

a

a

LEVEL 5

a	b	c

---

1 LISTENING

LEVEL 2

a	b	c	d	e

LEVEL 3

a	b	c	d

LEVEL 4

a	b	c	d

LEVEL 5

a	b	c	d	e

2 READING

LEVEL 2

a	b	c	d	e	f

LEVEL 3

a	b	c	d	e	f

LEVEL 4

a	b	c	d

LEVEL 5

a	b	c	d	e

3 WRITING

LEVEL 2

a	b	c	d

LEVEL 3

a	b	c	d	e

LEVEL 4

a	b	c	d	e

LEVEL 5

a	b	c	d	e

NAME _____

CLASS _____

© HIGHLIGHT ENGLISH

Acknowledgements

The author and publishers would like to thank the following for permission to reproduce copyright material:

Allen Cullen for extract from *John Willy and the Bee People*; Carcanet Press Ltd for 'The Computer's First Christmas Card' from *Collected Poems* by Edwin Morgan; British Rail for British Rail tickets; Metro Centre, Tyne and Wear, for Metro Centre tickets; Tyne Valley Coaches Ltd for bus tickets; Hamish Whitely for *The Red Apple* by Hamish Whitely.